DATE DUE

NOV 08 1983		
MAR 1 9 1987		
DEC 19 '92		

DEMCO 38-297

AMERICAN CITIES CHRONOLOGY SERIES

SAN FRANCISCO
A CHRONOLOGICAL & DOCUMENTARY HISTORY

1542- 1970

Compiled and Edited by
ROBERT⌊MAYER

Series Editor
HOWARD B. FURER

1974
OCEANA PUBLICATIONS, INC.
Dobbs Ferry, New York

Library of Congress Cataloging in Publication Data

Mayer, Robert, 1934-
    San Francisco: a chronological and documentary
history, 1542-1970.

    (American cities chronology series)
    SUMMARY: A chronological history of San Francisco
with selected pertinent documents.
    Bibliography: p.
    1. San Francisco-History--Chronology. 2. San
Francisco--History--Sources.   [1. San Francisco--His-
tory]   I. Title.
F869.S3M32   979.4'61   74-8846
ISBN 0-379-00614-6

TABLE OF CONTENTS

EDITOR'S FOREWORD.   v

CHRONOLOGY   1
   The Spanish Period, 1542-1821   1
   The Mexican Period, 1821-1846.   4
   American Possession and Organization 1846-1848   8
   The Gold Rush, 1848-1860   10
   Era of Industrialization, 1860-1900   20
   The Turn of the Century, 1900-1906   30
   The Earthquake and Reconstruction, 1906-1920.   31
   The 1920s   38
   Depression and Recovery, 1929-1941   40
   War and Peace, 1941-1952   43
   The Modern Period, 1952-1970   46

DOCUMENTS   53
   The Discovery of San Francisco Bay, 1774   54
   The Founding of San Francisco, 1776   55
   Description of Conditions in San Francisco, 1816   60
   Description of San Francisco by the Russian Explorer
      Otto von Kotzebue, 1824   61
   Description of San Francisco by Frederick William
      Beechey, 1825.   62
   An American Visit to San Francisco, 1825   63
   San Francisco in 1835   64
   Description of San Francisco, 1837   65
   The United States Takes Possession of San Francisco, 1846 . .   66
   The Naming of San Francisco by Alcalde Bartlett, January 23,
      1847   68
   Letter from Colonel R.B. Mason to George Hyde, July 15,
      1847   69
   The Laws of the Town of San Francisco, 1847   70
   The Gold Rush, 1848.   75
   First City Charter of San Francisco, 1850   76
   The Woman Problem, 1850   79
   The Fire of May 4, 1851   81
   The San Francisco Fire Department of 1851   82
   The Increase and Impunity of Crime, 1851   83
   The County Jail, 1851   85
   The Constitution of the First Vigilance Committee, 1851 . . .   86
   The Execution of Jenkins, June 10, 1851   87
   The Vigilance Committee of 1853   89

The Broderick-Terry Duel and The Slavery Issue,
    September, 1859. 92
The First Transcontinental Railroad, 1869 94
The Barbary Coast, 1875 95
The Chinese Problem, 1879 97
The Palace Hotel, 1875 98
A Poem for San Francisco, 1870s 100
The Cable Cars of San Francisco, 1889 101
Anti-Chinese Prejudice, 1897 102
Chinatown, 1900 103
The City Charter of 1900 105
The Great Earthquake, 1906 114
New York Times Report of the Earthquake, 1906 116
Proclamation by the Mayor Placing the City under Martial
    Law, 1906 119
Bubonic Plague, 1907 120
The Breaking of the Unions, 1916 122
The Pagoda-Like Phone Exchange, 1929 127
The City Charter of 1931 128
Opposition to the 1931 Charter by Vested Interests 132
Labor Violence, July 6, 1934 134
Recommendations of the City Planning Committee, 1965 137
The Hippie Subculture, 1967 139

BIBLIOGRAPHY 143

NAME INDEX 151

EDITOR'S FOREWORD

This book is a research tool compiled primarily for the student. It presents a basic chronology, and a sample of source documents of the city of San Francisco. The events and documents have been carefully selected to present a picture of the social, political, and economic conditions of the city, while maintaining the colorful flavor of what has been written about the city by the bay.

Every attempt has been made to cite the most accurate dates in this chronology. If there is an error, it is due to the fact that some of the sources conflict, and the more plausible date has been used.

A critical, comprehensive bibliography is also included in the hope that the interested student will investigate additional material. The sources include primary and secondary material.

Robert Mayer
Newark State College
Union, New Jersey

THE SPANISH PERIOD 1542-1821

1542   November 15. Portugese explorer, Juan Rodrigus Cabrillo
                was the first European to come to the vicinity of San Fran-
                cisco. While there is no record of Cabrillo discovering the
                Bay, he did record a group of islands twenty-seven miles
                west of San Francisco which were later named the Farallon
                Islands.

1579   June 17. Sir Francis Drake, the English explorer, passed
                San Francisco Bay and landed at what is now known as
                Drake's Bay a few miles northwest of San Francisco Bay.
                He named California "New Albion" and claimed it for Eng-
                land. This stirred Spain to continue exploring California
                to protect South American trade with Manila and the Orient.

1584   Possible sighting of San Francisco Bay by the Spanish ex-
                plorer Francisco Gali.

1585   January 22. Viceroy Pedro Moya y Contreras ordered an
                expedition to find a harbor on the California coast where
                ships plying the Orient trade could land and repair.

1595   November 5. Sebastian Rodrigues Cermeno, another Span-
                ish explorer, explored the region and probably landed at
                Drake's Bay. He gave it the name La Bahia de San Francis-
                co.

1603   The Conde de Monterey was made viceroy of Peru. Spanish
                exploration of California ceased for one hundred and sixty
                years, because his successor was opposed to the plans to
                find a California port for the Manila galleons. Thus Spain
                lost one hundred years, and when she finally decided to ex-
                plore and settle the region, it was too late to firmly estab-
                lish control. This paved the way for the eventual United
                States conquest of California.

1762   Catherine II came to the Russian throne, and started Rus-
                sian exploration, and the settlement of California. The
                Spanish became fearful that the Russians would expand south
                and threaten their Mexican settlements. That fear moti-
                vated the Spanish to start the explorations and mission chain
                that resulted in the founding of San Francisco in 1776.

1769   March 9. Gaspar de Portola, with an exploration party,
                left Loreto to take possession of California. His main pur-

pose was to prevent Russian expansion from the north which might threaten Spain's South American colonies. He also wanted to find a good harbor on the coast.

March 25. Father Junipero Serra, with two soldiers and a servant, set out on foot to overtake Portola.

October 31. The Portola expedition, camped beside San Pedro Creek, and saw San Francisco Bay. Portola sent Sergeant Ortega, and a detachment to explore the Bay and find a way around it.

November 2. Sergeant Jose Ortega reached San Francisco Bay.

1772   March 26. Pedro Fages and Father Crespi, on another exploration mission, saw the Golden Gate Strait from the east side of the Bay, and camped near what is now known as the University of California campus.

1775   August 5. Captain Juan Manuel de Ayala arrived off the Golden Gate in the ship San Carlos. He was exploring the region by the sea to make the area secure for Spain against the Russian threat. His orders instructed him to survey the bay. Alaya, finding this a better harbor than Drake's Bay, transferred the name San Francisco to that body. Thus, San Francisco got its name. However, during the Spanish period the town was called Yerba Buena.

1776   March 28. Juan Bautista de Anza, sent from Mexico to form a colony at San Francisco Bay, selected the site for the Presidio. This became the first settlement.

March 29. The site for the Mission San Francisco was selected by Father Francisco Palou.

September 17. Father Palou dedicated the Mission San Francisco de Assisi, later known as Mission Dolores. The Presidio was also dedicated by Lieutenant Jose Joaquin Morega on that day.

October 8. The first white baby was born at the Mission Dolores.

1777   June 1. The first Indian converts were baptized at the Mission.

1782   April 25. The cornerstone of the present Mission Dolores
was laid. It contained the image of St. Francis, some rel-
ics of the bones of St. Pius and other holy martyrs, five
medals of various saints, and a good portion of silver money to signify the treasures of the Church.

November 14. The English explorer George Vancouver,
sailed H.B.M. sloop-of-war <u>Discovery</u> into the Golden Gate
and anchored at a cove called El Paraje de Yerba Buena,
the Place of Good Herb. This was the first non-Spanish
ship to sail into the Bay. Vancouver set up a tent on the
shore, while he obtained supplies and established the first
shelter on the site of the future city.

1799   May 24. The American ship <u>Eliza</u>, hunting sea otters in
the Pacific, sailed into San Francisco Bay. This was the
first record of an American ship to visit the city.

1802   February 2. The first of many natural disasters which
were to plague the city occured; a storm destroyed most of
the roofs at the Presidio. The roofs and buildings were constructed of adobe which washed away when it rained. This
was one example of why the Spanish were never able to secure the region.

1806   April. Nicolai Petrovich Rezanov, Chamberlain of Czar
Alexander I, visited the city. Americans had become active
in the sea otter trade. The slaughter of large numbers of
these animals posed a threat to the Russians, and they were
trying to obtain supplies for their Alaskan colony. Also,
they attempted to ascertain the strength of the Spanish colony, in the event they (the Russians) wanted to move south.
The United States and Russia continued to test the Spanish
position and both countries looked for potential allies.

1808   Napoleon Bonaparte invaded Spain, imprisoned the royal
family and precipitated the many wars of independence in
South America.

The lack of firm civil authority in Mexico cut off the normal
supply of food and armaments to the Yerba Buena garrison,
and lowered their morale. This made it more susceptible
to take over by the United States.

June 21. The first earthquake was reported in San Francisco.

1811   Treaty between Russia and Spain allowed the Russians to
        hunt for sea otters in Spanish California. As Spain could
        not prevent Russian hunting off the California coast, they
        tried to form an alliance with them against the Americans.

1816   October 25. An international conference between Spain and
        Russia was held to try and settle the problem of Russian
        expansion into Spanish California. The conference was not
        able to settle the issue.

1820   The increased use of Yerba Buena cove as an anchorage dic-
        tated the site of the future city.

THE MEXICAN PERIOD 1821-1846

1821   September 27. Mexico achieved independence from Spain
        with California as part of the new republic, thus ending
        Spanish rule in that part of the world. This further isolated
        California and was another step in its transfer to the United
        States.

1824   Otto von Kotzebue, in the Russian frigate, Predpriatie,
        sailed into San Francisco Bay. Upon his return to Russia
        he published New Voyage Round the World, filled with glow-
        ing praise for San Francisco. The book did much to publi-
        cize the area and increase worldwide interest in the Cali-
        fornia port.

1825   Captain Benjamin Morrell visited Yerba Buena in the Ameri-
        can ship Tartar. Morrell wrote a travelog, Narrative of
        Four Voyages, which did much to increase American inter-
        est in the city and harbor.

1827   Governor Jose Maria Echeandia ordered Yerba Buena Cove
        guarded against smuggling. The Russians and the Ameri-
        cans landed goods at Yerba Buena to avoid customs in Mon-
        terey and Mexico. This problem was never solved during
        the Mexican period. Many ships put in at Yerba Buena be-
        cause of loose customs control, and thereby increased its
        traffic and settlement.

1828   Jedediah Smith, an American citizen, visited Yerba Buena.
        Impressed with its potential fur and ocean trade, he was
        one of the people who disseminated information about the
        bay to interested Americans, and to the Hudson's Bay Co.
        This helped sustain American interest in the future city.

1832   Thomas O. Larkin, who became the U.S. Consul at Monte-
       rey, reached California from New England, established
       himself as a prosperous merchant, and aroused American
       interest in the region by articles in Boston and New York
       newspapers.

1833   Mexico passed the secularization act, which turned over
       the mission-controlled land to private ownership. This act
       lessened church control and increased immigration to the
       city. It later caused a problem for the United States when
       title to the city passed from Mexico to the United States, be-
       cause of many conflicting claims for land and the incomplete-
       ness of the records.

1834   December 7. The legislative body of California brought
       about the first formal government in Yerba Buena consist-
       ing of an ayuntaminto, or council, composed of an alcalde
       or chief official, two regidores and a sindico-procurador.
       Twenty-seven men cast votes at the Presidio for eleven
       electors, who, in turn, selected new officials. Francisco
       de Haro was chosen first mayor under Mexican rule.

1835   January 1. The city government began to function. One of
       its first acts was to grant the 2200 acre Rancho Laguna de
       la Merced to Jose Galino.

       June 25. First permanent structure at Yerba Buena built by
       Captain A. Richardson, former mate on the English whaler
       Orion. The Mexican Government had appointed Richardson
       harbor master, attesting to the growing importance of the
       city.

       July 4. The American flag flew over the city for the first
       time at a celebration party given by two American citizens,
       Leese and Primer. They had come to Yerba Buena to trade,
       in order to avoid Mexican customs.

       September 29. Governor Figueroa died after a two year
       and nine month administration. He had been responsible for
       great changes in Yerba Buena, encouraged foreign com-
       merce and immigration, extended the Spanish frontier north
       of San Francisco Bay, and laid the foundation for the com-
       mercial city of Yerba Buena. Mexico's hold on California
       began to decline and the governors who followed did not have
       his political skill and foresight.

December 4. Richard Henry Dana, author of <u>Two Years</u>
<u>Before the Mast</u> first arrived in the city aboard the <u>Alert</u>.
His book did much to publicize the importance of Yerba
Buena in the United States.

President Jackson directed his Secretary of State to offer
$500,000 for San Francisco Bay and the area to the north.
The offer was not accepted by Mexico.

1836   Yerba Buena was now an important trading and smuggling
port. Telegraph Hill was settled, and the first house was
built by Widow Briones. Telegraph Hill was called Loma
Alta at the time, and was the third area settled in the city.
The Presidio and the Trading Post were the first sections
settled.

1838   The city government fell into disuse. The council ceased
to meet; alcaldes were elected regularly, but the duties
were light and the office was considered a means of honoring its holder. This was another example of the laxity of
the Mexican rule.

1839   The first town survey was ordered and completed. Alcalde
Francisco de Haro commissioned grocer and surveyor Vioget for the work. His map laid out streets and property
lines in the district bounded by the present Montgomery,
Sacramento, Dupont, and Pacific streets. Vioget did the
survey in checkerboard fashion, and did not follow the natural contour of the hills. His survey set the pattern and design for the future development of the city.

John Augustus Sutter, famous for the gold discovery in 1848,
sailed into San Francisco Bay on board the English brig,
<u>Clementine</u>.

1841   August 14. Official American interest in San Francisco Bay
began when the U.S. sloop-of-war, <u>Vincennes</u>, entered the
Golden Gate and anchored at Yerba Buena. It was commanded by Lieutenant Ringgold, under the general command of
Wilkes, who was exploring the Pacific coast in an attempt
to find an overland route to California.

1842   During the Webster-Ashburton negotiations, President Ty-
ler agreed to settle the issue on the line of the Columbia
River, if Britain would persuade Mexico to sell northern
California to the United States. The money would have

been used to reimburse British and American creditors. This scheme was not successful.

October 20. Commodore Jones, an American naval officer in the Pacific, believed war had broken out with Mexico. He went to Monterey, the capital of California, forced the Mexican authorities to surrender the fort, raised the American flag, and issued a proclamation of annexation. The next day he learned there was no war; he lowered the flag, made his apologies, boarded his ship and was relieved of his command, straining Mexican-American relations in the process.

1844

The Governor at Monterey ordered construction of the Custom House, the first government owned building. This was another attempt to prevent the widespread smuggling. Like the other measures, the Custom House had little effect on the smuggling.

1845

The Polk Correlary to the Monroe Doctrine was announced, reflecting fears that Britain wanted to possess California. Fear of the British obtaining California was one of the factors that precipitated the Mexican war.

June. Governor Don Pio Pico, last Mexican governor of California, ordered the sale of the land belonging to the Mission Dolores.

Secretary of the U.S. Navy, George Bancroft, instructed Commodore John D. Sloat, commander of the Pacific Squadron, to seize San Francisco harbor and other California ports in the event of war with Mexico.

There was a second town survey. Alcalde Jose Sanchez ordered extension of existing streets and addition of new ones to the Vioget survey. A new map was to be drawn and the area of the town increased. The map doubled the size of the town, and was kept behind the bar of Robert Ridley on Kearny Street. The names of property owners were merely written on the map, and changes made directly thereon. This caused much legal confusion at a later date.

October 17. President Polk appointed John Slidell U.S. Consul at Monterey, with confidential instructions to counteract foreign influences, stimulate separatist tendencies, and encourage Californian annexation to the United States.

1846   Spring. Fremont started a local revolt, the Bear Flag Re-
                volution, against Mexico in the vicinity of San Francisco
                Bay.

                May 11. President Polk sent his message to Congress de-
                claring war on Mexico.

                July. Fremont received unofficial news that the United
                States and Mexico were at war, and cooperated with Com-
                modore Sloat and Captain Robert F. Stockton of the U.S.
                Navy for the occupation of all of California.

                July 8. Official news was received that the United States
                and Mexico were at war.

                Captain Montgomery received orders to occupy Yerba Buena
                and adjacent regions.

AMERICAN POSSESSION AND ORGANIZATION 1846-1848

                July 9. Montgomery landed at Yerba Buena with weventy
                men and encountered no opposition. At 8 A.M. the United
                States flag was raised in the plaza in front of the custom
                house. A twenty-one gun salute from the Portsmouth pro-
                claimed that the city was in the possession of the United
                States.

                Population of Yerba Buena at the time of the conquest was
                less than 400.

                July 29. Elder Sam Brannan and one hundred and fifty Mor-
                mons sailed into Yerba Buena Cove from New York to settle
                in San Francisco Bay.

                August 6. Captain Montgomery formed the first American
                government in San Francisco by appointing Lieutenant Alan
                Bartlett of the United States Navy, mayor of the city.

                September 15. To legalize the above action, an election
                was held which confirmed Bartlett's appointment.

1847   January 9. Sam Brannan started the first newspaper in Cali-
                fornia at San Francisco and called it the California Star.
                It was published weekly.

                The first private school was started by J.D. Marston.

The first Sunday School was started by Methodist Missionaries.

January 30. Mayor Bartlett issued an ordinance which
changed the name of the city from Yerba Buena to San Francisco.

February. Word reached San Francisco that the Donner
party of eighty-seven men, women, and children, attempt-
ing to reach the city over the Sierras was snowbound. Vol-
unteers formed, and four separate relief parties went out.
Less than fifty of the original eighty-seven finally reach
San Francisco.

February 22. Edwin Bryant became Alcalde.

March 3. Recognizing the isolated nature of the outpost,
and the need for better communication between the East
Coast and San Francisco, Congress authorized the secretary of the navy to advertise bids for steamships to operate
on both oceans, with a crossing at Panama. The ships were
to be subsidized by carrying mail. They were also authorized to carry passengers and freight. This was the beginning of the end of California isolation and the reaffirmation
of San Francisco as the major West Coast port.

May. George Hyde was appointed Alcalde.

August. First formal municipal government of San Francisco was formed. It was composed of a mayor and town
council. American alcaldes had previously served without
council. The legal base was an order from the governor of
California to the Alcalde of San Francisco directing him to
form an ayuntamiento to aid him in administering the growing settlement.

August 15. A second newspaper, the <u>Californian</u> was formed.

Washington A. Bartlett, the Alcalde, ordered Jasper O'Farrell to make the first American survey of the town. O'Farrell wanted to map the town according to the natural hilly
terrain but the Alcalde and citizens insisted upon a hard-
and-fast gridiron layout to give the maximum profits upon
subdivision. O'Farrell did this by following the Vioget survey, and extending it to increase the area of the town by
800 acres. His only creativity was Market Street, which

intersected the gridiron at an angle from the cove to the
Mission, thus dividing the town and causing a crosstown
traffic problem which exists today. O'Farrell also gave
the streets their present names, using the names of men
who had been prominent in California before the American
conquest.

THE GOLD RUSH - 1848-1860

1848   The population of San Francisco was 900 people.

January 24. There were a series of fortunate accidents
that caused San Francisco to grow from a sleepy port to a
major, booming American metropolis. James Marshall
picked up a few flakes of yellow metal from the tailrace of
Captain John A. Sutter's new sawmill on the American River. When news of the discovery of gold hit the town, the
population dropped to twelve people.

February 2. Treaty of Guadalupe Hidalgo formally ended
the war with Mexico and legalized the American possession
of California, including San Francisco.

March 15. First printed notice about the discovery of gold
appeared in the Californian.

March 18. The California Star, a weekly paper, printed a
similar short account. These notices caused no excitement.

May. Sam Brannan started the actual gold rush when he ex-
hibited a bottle of gold dust that he had picked up on his
visit to the American River.

Spring. All town newspapers suspended publication due to
the gold rush.

July 25. Colonel Richard Mason, military governor of California, issued a proclamation asking public cooperation in
apprehending deserters because of the gold rush. He also
granted liberal furloughs to the soldiers so that they might
visit the gold field. These measures were not effective.

Fall. First of a series of governmental and electoral problems developed in San Francisco. Six councilmen were to
be elected to serve until successors could be chosen at a
later election. The election was disputed and six additional

elections were held by August 11, 1849. The Governor, the alcalde, the first council, and the elected council each disputed as to who had the authority to run the city.

October. The 150 ton steamer California sailed from New York to San Francisco to inaugurate steamship travel between the east and west coasts.

December 24. The first of a series of disastrous fires, which were to plague the city, groke out. They caused one million dollars in damage, mainly to the gambling and entertainment section of the city. There were three causes for the fires: accidents; hasty, faulty, and inflammable construction; and arson by gangs, in order to create a diversion while they looted the city.

1849   January. The fire department was organized in San Francisco at a mass meeting in Portsmouth Square. Three engine companies were formed, the San Francisco, the Empire, and the Protection. They were volunteer companies, as was the practice, and funds were raised to purchase the necessary equipment and to provide quarters for it.

February 28. The Pacific Mail Company's steamer California passed through the Golden Gate.

May. The Town council appropriated funds for combating the fires which were becoming a menace. They were to use the funds for digging additional wells and building a reservoir. Two ordinances were passed directing property owners to keep six buckets full of water on hand at all times. Heavy fines were to be levied on those who refused to fight fires, or refused to remove property in the path of fires. The ordinance also prohibited building of houses made of canvas, one of the reasons that fires spread so rapidly.

May. The San Francisco Wharf Association, a group of city merchants, was organized to build a new series of piers for handling the tremendous increase in shipping that the gold rush and rapid growth of the city had caused. Two miles of piers, costing one and a half million dollars, were constructed within a year and a half.

May 4. Second great fire in San Francisco caused three million dollars worth of damage to the merchant and banking section of the city.

Summer: First racial and civil disturbances were reported
in the city. Gangs of people from New York and Australia
formed an organization called the "Hounds." With the slo-
gan, "San Francisco for the Americans," they thought it
their civic duty to eliminate the Spanish-speaking population.
On July 15 the "Hounds" attacked Spanish-Town, destroying
the entire colony and shooting the occupants as they fled.
The counter-reaction included W. E. Spofford's organizing
230 citizens to act as a police force, which, on July 16 arrested and imprisoned twenty "Hounds" aboard the U.S.S.
Warren. They were tried, convicted, and sent out of the
country. It was the first of many such vigilance committees
that took over the city in times of civic unrest, working outside of the law to maintain law and order.

July 6. Commander Sloat issued a proclamation that all
land grants given by the Mexican government would be hon-
ored by the American government. The treaty of Guadalupe-
Hidalgo reaffirmed this promise.

August. Alcalde John W. Geary stated that the town was
broke. There were no police or jails in the city. Public
improvements were unknown, and the city could not protect
property, maintain order, or promote properity. To remedy the situation, Alcalde Geary increased the license fees
charged gamblers, which became the city's largest source
of revenue. He also established a municipal court, organized a paid police force, and purchased the brig Euphemia
to be used as a city jail.

Fall. The Californian and the California Star merged and
became the Alta California.

November. There were five hundred abandoned ships in
the harbor because of the gold rush.

Winter. The "Hounds" kept disturbing the city with nightly
forays. Their headquarters were near Portsmouth Square.
They would attack, beat, rob and set fire to the foreigners'
houses.

1850   January 1. The population of San Francisco was 35,000.

The Chinese population of the city was 787.

The first ferry service was inaugurated to Oakland by two

Alameda County residents named Carpenter and Moon. They converted an old lumber schooner named the <u>Kangaroo</u> into a ferry boat, which made two trips weekly.

A new type of building was constructed in the city because of the devastating effect that the fires had on the old ones. This type was to remain a characteristic of the business district for many years. They were narrow, two and three story brick houses, with iron shutters in front of the doors and windows. The shutters could be opened in the day for business, and closed at night to secure the building against vandalism and fire, both of which were prevalent in the booming town.

Spring. Bavarian-born Levi Strauss, creator of "Levis" arrived in the city with a supply of clothing and dry goods to open up a business.

April. The first theater in the city opened.

The first free public school in the state of California was financed by, and opened in San Francisco.

April 15. The first city charter was enacted.

May. California was admitted to the Union.

May 1. The San Francisco Chamber of Commerce was organized. Beverly Sanders was the first president.

June 14. Third disastrous fire lasted three days and consumed five million dollars worth of buildings and goods. The business district and waterfront were the victims of the fire.

September 9. The president signed a bill admitting California to the Union.

September 17. Fire destroyed one hundred and twenty-five buildings with resulting looting and lawlessness.

October 19. The mail steamer <u>Oregon</u> entered the Golden Gate bringing the news that California had been admitted to the Union.

November 6. President Millard Fillmore recognized the

need to build adequate defenses for the outpost of the empire on the Pacific. He reserved Angel and Yerba Islands, and Point San Jose for military purposes.

1851   The first institute of higher education in the San Francisco area was formed when Archbishop Joseph Sadoc Alemany gave funds to Reverend John Nobili to establish a college in the abandoned Mission Santa Clara. The school received a charter in 1855 and is now the University of Santa Clara.

The second city charter was adopted.

February 19. The editorial in the Alta California cried to clean up the lawlessness caused by the gold, and mass influx of people. This precipitated the next vigilance committee.

May 1. The heart of the city was burned out by another great fire, the fifth and largest fire the city had experienced since the beginning of the gold rush. It caused seven million dollars in property damage.

The people felt the fire was caused by incendiaries who wanted to create a diversion while they robbed and looted the city. This feeling was increased by editorials in the newspapers, which urged that committees of safety be organized to halt further entrance into the city of foreigners from Australia, and to clear the city of all doubtful characters.

June. Another great fire completed the destruction of what had been spared by the first blaze.

June 6. A county jail was constructed to replace the prison on ship Euphemia.

June 7. Report by the chief engineer to the city council stated that the apparatus and houses of the fire department were inadequate and unusable due to the fire. The city treasury was also empty.

June 9. A vigilance committee was organized to keep law and order in San Francisco. It was composed of about two hundred people who attempted to enlarge the committee by including business and professional people from neighboring communities.

June 11. For the first time, a man was publicly lynched in San Francisco by the vigilance committee. He was accused of stealing a small safe containing $1500 from the office of a Mr. Virgin, and, was apprehended while trying to row across the bay.

June 12. At an inquest against the vigilance committee a coroner's jury condemned their action, and held nine of its members for the death of the man. The committee won popular support by stating they were all responsible. This, plus the prominent names attached to the document, won them wide support in the city, and they were not prosecuted.

July 11. The committee imposed the death penalty on James Stuart, a former convict from Sydney. He was found guilty of murder and executed on one of the wharves. The opponents of the committee tried to have the leaders indicted, but that failed. They then appealed to the governor at Sacramento.

August 18. The committee again acted against two suspected burglars, Samuel Whittaker and Robert McKenzie. After a test of strength with the local authorities when the prisoners were taken to the local jail, the committee broke into the jail and hung the two men. This was the last action of the committee. During their reign they hung three men, forced scores of "undesirables" to flee the city, and prevented the landing of many others. It could be argued that they drew attention to the weakness of the existing law enforcement agencies and caused new ones to be formed.

September. A common school system was adopted and a Board of Education appointed.

December. A rebuilding program, due to the fires, was undertaken. It included filling in of the tidelands between the shores and the piers. The sand was taken from the surrounding hills, the former crescent-shaped cove was filled in, land reclaimed and the piers replaced with streets that extended to the water front, thus giving the present configuration of the San Francisco waterfront.

1852   The city purchased for $200,000 the Jenny Lind Theater at Kearny and Washington Streets, and converted it into a city hall and court house. Civic improvements took place during that year including, laying of a three-mile long plank

road out Folsom Street to the Mission, the improvement of
port facilities, new churches, schools, theaters, founding
of a library, the building of the first horse-drawn streetcar
line and the formation of the San Francisco Gas Company.

Andrew S. Hallidie arrived from London. He was later to
invent the cable car.

The Chinese population in the city had reached 4,000. This
rapid increase in three years was to cause the racial problems that characterized the latter half of the century. The
first Chinese came in during the gold rush period. The later indlux was due to the heavy railroad construction.

October 28. San Francisco received some international fame
fame when William Walker, a citizen of the city, set out to
conquer part of Mexico, and initiate his South American fili-
bustering campaign.

1853   Congress recognized the importance of the West Coast city
and its lack of defense by appropriating $500,000 to fortify
the entrance to the Bay.

The city streets were lit by gas.

December. San Francisco boasted twelve daily newspapers,
six weeklies, and two tri-weekly papers. One tri-weekly
paper was French and the other one was German, which at-
tested to the city's cosmopolitan population.

1854   Construction began on the first light in the bay, located on
Alcatraz Island.

The first railroad was constructed in the city by Theodore
Dehone Judah, the engineer of the Erie Canal.

The three-story custom house at Battery, Washington, and
Jackson Streets was constructed. It housed the post office
and other federal offices.

Spring. Start of the first recorded depression in the city's
history. It was caused by declining gold production and
marked the end of the five-year boom the city had experienced since the discovery of gold.

The clipper ship, Flying Cloud made the journey from New

York to San Francisco in eighty-nine days, an all-time record for a crossing around-the-horn.

October 6. The section now known as the north beach and
fisherman's wharf was developed. "Honest" Harry Meiggs
did this by constructing a road around the base of the hill
paid for by a book of blank warrants signed by the mayor.
When the fraud became known, Meiggs went to Chile leaving
behind $800,000 in liabilities.

1855   Completion of the Panama Railroad across the Isthmus
eliminated most of the delays and hazards of the trip from
the East to the West Coast.

January. One-third of the city's 1,000 stores were vacant
due to the depression.

The first Chinese exclusion act was passed by the State Legislature.

Autumn. A committee was organized to combat the depression that had caused bank failures and left the city treasury
with a deficit of $840,000. They repudiated over a million
and a half of the city debts, thus putting San Francisco in
the black.

October 15. St. Ignatius Academy, San Francisco's first
institution of higher education, opened at the corner of Market and Stockton Streets. It later became the University of
San Francisco.

1856   The first public high school in California was established
in San Francisco.

April. The State Legislature provided for the consolidation
of city and county governments in San Francisco. It disposed of all city officials except the mayor, who appointed
the police judge, the marshal, the chief of police and the
board of education. He governed the city with justices of
the peace until the election in November, when a board of
supervisors was created. This form of government lasted
for forty-four years.

May 14. James P. Casey, editor of the Sunday Times, shot
James King, editor and founder of The Bulletin, who had
been denouncing Casey and others for ballot stuffing.

An outcry for a vigilance committee was again heard in the
city and citizens demanded that Casey be turned over to
them. A mass meeting was held on Battery Street, but no
decision was reached.

May 15. At a meeting on Sacramento Street in a building
fortified with sand bags, later known as Fort Gunnybanks,
a vigilance committee was formed with the merchant William T. Coleman as chairman. Twenty-five hundred men
were enrolled and equipped with arms.

May 16. Governor J. Neely Johnson arrived from Sacramento and urged the vigilantes to disband. They refused.

May 18. The committee ordered Casey and another prisoner,
Charles Cora, to be taken from jail and brought before them
for trial.

May 19. The vigilantes marched on the jail and took possession of the prisoners, who were tried, convicted of murder,
and sentenced to be hanged.

May 22. King was given an impressive funeral and the prisoners were hung from a gallows at Fort Gunnybags.

The committee searched the city for all "law breakers,"
and forced them out of the country.

June 3. The governor declared San Francisco in a state of
insurrection.

July 18. The committee assembled, held a parade, and disbanded. The result of their patrolling the city day and night
was the deportation of twenty-five "dangerous criminals,"
the voluntary exit of eight hundred others, and the trial and
execution of four men.

December 1. The Morning Call was first published. It was
named for a popular play of the time by George E. Barnes.

1857

Congress passed a bill granting a subsidy to the Butterfield
Overland Stage Company to carry the mail between St. Louis
and San Francisco. Thus, reasonably priced, fast and de-
pendable mail service was inaugurated. At its peak, the
organization had a thousand employees and more than one
hundred Concord Coaches. Working with a subsidy of

$600,000 a year, they carried both passengers and mail. The service proved to be unsatisfactory to the San Franciscans, because the stages followed the southern route and was no faster than the Panama steamers. The residents, therefore, joined those in Sacramento, Salt Lake City, and other communities, in urging the Federal Government to subsidize a second line along the central route. The pressure resulted in the formation of the Pony Express in 1860.

The first Chinese place of worship in the United States, the Kong Chow Temple on Pine Street, was built.

September. The first fair in San Francisco was held by the Mechanics Institute, in conjunction with the California Horticultural Society. It was an agricultural fair displaying fruits, flowers, and products of the vines. It demonstrated the richness of the soil, and helped publicize California agriculture which drew more settlers.

1858   A gold strike in British Columbia solved the unemployment problems.

The city emptied for another gold rush.

June. The first reform school was established for the retraining of juvenile delinquents.

1859   Herbert Howe Bancroft, a San Francisco bookseller started collecting volumes about the West. This library became the famous Bancroft Collection purchased by the University of California at Berkeley for $25,000 in 1905. The library now has over four million books.

Spring. Huge deposits of silver-nitrate ore were discovered on the slopes of Sun Mountain in the Sierras. This was the famous Comstock lode and created another mass exodus from the city; this time a silver rush. During the next twenty years the mines produced well over $300,000,000, much of which went to San Francisco, whose citizens controlled major portions of the mines and financed their development. Aside from profiting the city in general, the mines produced the city's first multi-millionaires.

Summer. Richard Henry Dana returned to San Francisco aboard the Pacific Mail steamer Golden Gate from Panama. Again he wrote about the city, noting its changes in twenty-four years.

ERA OF INDUSTRIALIZATION 1860-1900

1860   A literary movement of considerable force and originality
            flourished in the 1860's. Among the writers in town were
            Mark Twain, Bret Harte, Ambrose Bierce, Henry George,
            and a host of lesser lights. In a sense, it was a literary
            rebellion against the proper Bostonian standards and tastes
            of the East.

            The San Francisco and San Jose Railroad, first railroad in
            the city, was organized.

            January 1. The population of San Francisco was 56,880.

            April 3. The first Pony Express rider left St. Joseph, Mis-
            souri for Sacramento, California. The service was insti-
            tuted due to pressure from San Francisco for a faster mail
            service than the Butterfield Stage provided. The two thou-
            sand mile trip was made in ten and a half days, the riders
            changing horses every twenty-five miles. Two round trips
            were made each week and a letter cost $5.00 per one-half
            ounce.

            July 4. Service started on the city's first street railroad,
            the San Francisco Market Street Railroad Company.

1861   April 24. The War Department sent General E. V. Sumner
            to San Francisco to take over command of the Department
            of the Pacific. He replaced Brigadier General Albert Sidney
            Johnston, a Southerner, whose loyalty to the Union was ques-
            tioned. The command passed without a problem, and helped
            California remain loyal to the Union during the war.

            The news of the firing on Fort Sumter reached the city via
            Pony Express and was greeted by an upsurge of patriotism.

            May 1. The city authorized construction of a railroad be-
            tween Oakland and San Francisco. It was planned to span
            the water by bridge to Yerba Buena Island and proceed by
            ferry from there to the city.

            June 28. The Central Pacific Railroad Company was organ-
            ized by four Sacramento shopkeepers, Collis Huntington,
            Charles Crocker, Mark Hopkins and Leland Stanford. The
            railroad finally linked the city with the east coast, and helped
            build it into a metropolis. The railroad was also to become

an influential and controlling factor in San Francisco and
State politics.

September 8. The Stock Exchange Board was created, deal-
ing mainly in silver stocks.

October 26. The final link in the wires of the overland telegraph system across the continent was completed. San
Francisco was thus electronically linked with the East. A
casualty was the romantic Pony Express, which was phased
out.

1862   Winter. Congress passed the Pacific Railroad bill, which
authorized the building of a railroad between Sacramento
and the Missouri River. The contract for the western half
of the road was given to the Central Pacific Railroad Company, which was succeeded by the Southern Pacific.

1863   The Democratic Press started publication. It later became
the San Francisco Examiner.

The San Francisco and San Jose Railroad was completed to
Big Tree Station at Palo Alto.

A massive civic improvement program was undertaken,
which included a program of street repair and sidewalk
building. The streets were paved with wood. cobblestones,
and wooden blocks on a base of asphalt.

July 21. A Normal School opened on Powell Street with six
students. In 1870 it was moved to San Jose and became the
first of the state colleges.

October 23. Another periodic great fire broke out, and destroyed a major section of the financial district in the vicinity of Davis, California, and Sacramento streets.

Fall. Russian Navy ships visited San Francisco. This was
interpreted by the United States as a friendly gesture by the
Russians, especially since the sailors helped put out the
fire of October 23.

November. The Central Pacific bond issue was carried by
the voters, but by such a narrow margin, amidst charges of
bribery, that the Board of Supervisors refused to issue the
bonds. A strange compromise was agreed upon, and the city
made an outright gift of $450,000 to the railroad company.

1864   The profit from the silver mines caused a building boom. One thousand new buildings were built in 1864.

The first professional medical school, Tolard Medical College on Stockton Street was established.

May. Mark Twain moved to San Francisco at the age of twenty-eight.

November. San Francisco cast 21,024 votes for Abraham Lincoln, an overwhelming majority; more votes than the city of Boston cast, which was twice its size.

The San Francisco and San Jose Railroad was completed to San Jose.

1865   January 16. The Daily Dramatic Chronicle first appeared. It was later renamed the Morning Chronicle.

August 2. The first railroad locomotive built in California was constructed by Donahue, Booth and Co. at the Union Iron Works of San Francisco, and aptly named the "California."

1866   The Bank of California moved to California and Sansone streets.

The Merchants Exchange Building was completed, which firmly established California Street as the financial center of the West Coast.

November. The citizens voted to disband the volunteer fire companies on the grounds that they had achieved too much political power. A paid fire department was formed in their place.

1868   March 23. Governor Haight signed the bill which created the University of California at Berkeley.

1869   Emperor Norton I, an eccentric character of San Francisco, issued a proclamation commanding that a bridge be built across the Bay.

April 20. The transcontinental railroad was completed by the driving in of a golden spike at Promontory Point, Utah. San Francisco was now firmly linked with the East by fast steamer, telegraph and railroad. However, the railroad terminated in Sacramento and not San Francisco; a fact that created problems for many years.

The completion of the railroad threw 1,400 Chinese coolies out of work and onto the San Francisco labor market.

1870   The population of the city was 137,419.

The San Francisco and San Francisco and San Jose Railroad was completed to Gilroy.

The San Francisco, North Pacific, and the North Pacific Coast Railroad, extending to the Russian River in the communities of Marin, Sonoma and Mendocino Counties was constructed. The road terminated on the Marin Shore, and the passengers had to use a ferry to reach San Francisco.

Another program of street repair was undertaken.

This period also saw the construction of city facilities such as new schools and firehouses.

The construction of Golden Gate Park was started.

October 12. The Central Pacific gained control of the San Francisco and San Jose Railroad, and the Southern Pacific Railroad. These were organized into the Southern Pacific Railroad Company forming a railroad monopoly in California.

1871   Work started on a new city hall. It was planned to be the largest in the United States, a symbol of the way the citizens viewed their city. The construction was slowed down by corruption and other problems, and it took twenty-five years to complete. It was destroyed by the earthquake of 1906.

The stock market crashed and wiped out $60,000,000 in paper profits.

1872   The San Francisco Board of Education adopted a resolution providing separate schools for Orientals. This was part of the movement to exclude Japanese from the United States.

1873   January 28. The first of the famous San Francisco cable cars was installed. The first run was six blocks from Clay

and Kearny Streets to Jones Street. The cars were the
first real solution to climbing the steep hills of the city.
Their installation doubled real estate values on the hills,
and allowed the growth of the city westward toward the Presidio.

A medical school was established in San Francisco. This
was the first off-campus extension of the University of California.

October. Additional cable cars were installed in the city.

1874   There was a stock market boom based on the silver mines.

1875   The Pacific Mail Steamship Company opened regular service from San Francisco to Hawaii and the British Colonies
in the Orient.

January 30. Reciprocity treaty between the United States
and Hawaii was signed. The treaty caused an increase in
trade between Hawaii and San Francisco, which added to the
city's prosperity and growth.

August 26. The Bank of California shut its doors due to the
financial crash which hit the city.

October 14. The Palace Hotel opened on two acres of land.
It was truly palatial, boasting, among other things, 9,000
cuspidors, and space four times too large for the needs of
the city.

November. Leaders of anti-Chinese forces organized a
workingman's party. Almost their entire slate of candidates
was successful.

December 4. Mayor Andrew J. Bryant took office. He and
other anti-Chinese members of the government passed a
number of highly restrictive measures against the Chinese.
The anti-Chinese legislation included: an increase in license fees charged to Chinese businessmen; laws requiting
laundries to operate in fireproof buildings; a 2 a.m. curfew
applying to Chinese; prohibition of Chinese peddlers from
walking on sidewalks; more stringent housing and health regulations in Chinese quarter; and heavy fines against Chinese
convicted of gambling and opium smoking. Most of these
measures were loosely enforced; and ruled unconstitutional

by state and federal courts. The gambling and opium regulations proved impossible to enforce.

1876   The city was in a full scale depression; crops failed; the
gold and silver mines were running out, and railroad shipping fell off. The hardships of the recession increased anti-
Chinese resentment. The Chinese worked for less money
and thus were blamed for the unemployment.

Dennis D. Kearney led an army of unemployed in anti-Chinese riots. The riots started when a contractor replaced
white labor with Chinese, and the unemployed blamed their
plight on the Chinese rather than country-wide economic
conditions. The effects of the riot were one Chinese dead,
fifteen wounded, and their tent village burned to the ground.
Periodic riots characterized race relations until the Chinese
Exclusion Act was signed by Theodore Roosevelt on April
2, 1902.

1877   The Conservatory in Golden Gate Park is constructed. It
was a gift of the Crocker family and is still standing.

June. The Workingman's Party, which was anti-Chinese,
gained control of the State Constitutional Convention.

July 23. Anti-Chinese agitation again brok civilized bounds.
A Chinese laundry was burned to ashes and others were
sacked.

July 24. Mayor Bryant issued a proclamation stating that
the police had been ordered to suppress further violence.
A plea by the city press, clergy, and others for moderation
by the workers went unheeded.

July 25. Five thousand jobless workers were assembled for
a mass meeting and a fiery speech by d'Arcy. The mob,
out of control, went to Chinatown to stone and beat all the
Chinese they encountered.

July 26. The citizens formed another vigilance committee
called the Committee of Safety with William T. Coleman in
charge. They joined the police, encountered the rioters,
and a battle ensued. The vigilance committee eventually
numbered 5,438 men.

Mayor Bryant issued an order which prohibited public assem-

was issued

blages, and imposed a curfew from 10 P.M. to dawn. The
local authorities armed the Committee of Safety. Marines
from the Naval ships <u>Pensacola</u> and <u>Lancaster</u> were ready
to disembark. The U.S. Army provided 1,200 soldiers to
help local authorities. Armed patrols dispersed the crowds,
the riot was ended, and the Committee disbanded.

Fall. The Murphy Riot Act, which made it illegal to incite
a riot, was passed by the State Legislature in an effort to
control the periodic outbreaks in San Francisco.

1878   Second cable car line was completed to connect the financial
district with Nob Hill.

Slack times returned to the city causing a serious business
decline, and another rise in the number of unemployed.
The city speeded up its building program to compensate for
the construction slack.

The <u>San Francisco Chronicle</u> building was lighted by electricity.

1879   The California Electric Light Company of San Francisco,
probably the first company in the world to sell electrical
service, was formed.

1880   This decade was characterized by anti-Chinese and labor
agitation.

May 5. Mayor Kalloch was impeached for graft and corruption. *in gout*

1881   September 3. The courts declared the anti-Chinese ordinances invalid.

1882   An agreement was reached between Washington and Peking
to reduce the yearly quota of Chinese immigrants. This
was an attempt to solve the California racial problem.

1883   March 6. A new city charter was defeated.

1885   The first effective longshoreman's union, the Coast Sea-
man's Union, was formed. It was composed of the crews
of sailing ships engaged in coastal and inland trade. It became the focus for a powerful west coast longshoreman's
union, which dominated the labor politics of the next century.

Burnett Haskell tried to consolidate all the city's workers
into a single union and failed.

Twelve hundred members of the Iron Trades Council walked
out on strike as a result of the organization of the Federated
Trades Union, a state-wide union organization, which
pressed for better hours, recognition and salary.

1885   November. Chris Buckley, the so-called Blind Boss, and
his entire slate of candidates were elected in a municipal
election. He thus became the man to see for legitimate
and illegitimate buisness. He controlled the city government for almost ten years.

1886   May 18. Labor agitation led to the arrest of Socialist leaders.

1889   J.W. Stanford drove the first automobile, a new Winton, in
San Francisco.

June 6. A prize fight between James J. Corbett of San Francisco and Joe Choyniski was held on a barge in the bay.

1890   The population of San Francisco reached 298,997. The city
was eighth in size among the cities of the nation, and the
largest on the West Coast. It was second only to New York
in terms of foreign and domestic trade.

William Matson organized the Matson Naval Company, and
assembled a fleet of sailing ships for use in the Hawaiian-
San Francisco trade.

June 2. Anti-Chinese ordinances were again passed.

1891   The Steamshipmen's Union combined with the Coast Sea-
men's Union, and became the strongest maritime union in
the country with a membership of 4,000.

Summer. The Steam and Sailing Unions went on strike, and
brought on the bitterest labor-management struggle in the
city's history up to that time.

July 3. The Army of the Pacific, which had been based at
the Presidio, was abolished due to the ending of the Indian
Wars. The military command on the West Coast was decen-
tralized, divided among the Department of Arizona, the De-

partment of the Columbia, and the Department of California. The headquarters of the latter were at the Presidio.

November. The Socialist Labor party made its first try for election in the city.

The San Francisco Chronicle Building, the first steel-frame structure in the city, which was ten stories high, was completed.

1892   September 7. James J. Corbett of San Francisco knocked out John L. Sullivan in twenty-one rounds for the world championship of boxing.

1893   June 22. The Pacific Bank failed, starting the depression of 1893 in the city.

October 1. Labor riots broke out on the docks.

1894   The California Mid-Winter Exposition was held at Golden Gate Park.

November. Adolph Sutro, Populist Party candidate, was elected mayor. This represented the high point of the movement in San Francisco, and was the beginning of a period of responsible government for the city. He was a progressive reformer. His civic accomplishments included Parnassus Heights, the Cliff House, Sutro Heights, Sutro Baths, Sutro Forest and the famous Sutro Library.

1896   James Duval Phelan became the reform mayor. He gave the city a new charter, forced the gas rates down, and sponsored many programs to beautify and improve the city.

The new city charter, among other things, gave the mayor the power to appoint or remove from office the police commission, the board of health, and most other important boards and officers.

Gold was discovered in Alaska.

1897   July 15. The San Francisco Chronicle finally printed news of the discovery of gold in the Klondike. This official verification started the gold rush and introduced another boom period for the city.

Virginia Barstow was made city editor of the <u>Bulletin,</u> and became the first woman in the United States to hold such a position on a metropolitan newspaper.

The local architect, B.J.S. Cahill, was invited to submit a plan to beautify the city by efficient municipal planning of the civic center. His plan called for enlarging the area around the city hall, adding other public buildings, and creating an architecturally harmonious center set in handsomely landscaped grounds. The plan was judged too costly, and not adopted. However, it gave impetus to a "city beautiful" movement which was later fulfilled.

1898

A new city charter was voted upon to replace the charter of 1896. Ironically, this charter placed the city under a more corrupt regime than the one it was supposed to supercede.

March 12. The <u>Oregon</u> sailed from San Francisco Bay on its famous run around South America to join the U.S. Atlantic fleet.

April. Harbor defenses were increased due to the Spanish-American War.

May 4. President McKinley signed an order for troops to be assembled in San Francisco, which made it the major American base for U.S. Asiatic operations during the Spanish-American War. The city became an embarkation and naval port for troops which were to occupy and quell the insurrection in the Philippines. This aided prosperity and growth.

May 26. The new City Charter was ratified.

November. Construction of the San Francisco Ferry Building to handle the immense bay traffic was completed. At the height of the ferryboat era, fifty million passengers passed through the building each year. London's Charing Cross Station was the only depot in the world to accomodate a larger number.

1899

San Francisco State College was founded.

THE TURN OF THE CENTURY
1900-1906

1900   The first Japanese exclusion meeting was held in San Fran-
                cisco.

                The population of San Francisco was over 400,000, and the
                architectural configuration of the city began to change; the
                wooden structures were replaced by buildings of steel and
                concrete.

                November. The Freeholder's charter was accepted and
                stood until 1931. The major features allowed for municipal
                ownership of utilities and civil services, including public
                utilities, waterworks, street and railroad systems. The
                city was now able to assume control of all these vital ser-
                vices.

1901   Mayor Phelan appointed a committee to survey the Sierra
                Nevada range and find a suitable spot to obtain additional
                water for the city. Opposition to this plan by conservation-
                ists, mountain men, and other groups prevented it from be-
                coming a reality until 1913 when Congressional opposition
                ceased.

                Spring. Several thousand workers in the metal trade indus-
                tries formed a union and went on strike. The strike be-
                came a test of strength between labor and management.
                Management formed their own organization, the Employers
                Alliance, which put pressure on other shop owners to stop
                the formation of unions.

                Restaurant employees walked out and caused another con-
                frontation with the Employers Alliance. The truckers'
                union then struck, threatening to paralyze the city. When
                non-union drivers were hired, rioting and warfare broke
                out.

                July 30. Thirteen thousand longshoremen, warehouse work-
                ers, sailors, and shipbuilders struck causing a complete
                economic standstill.

                October. Governor Henry T. Gage announced that unless
                the strike was settled voluntarily, he would call out the Na-
                tional Guard to patrol the streets and restore order. This
                threat settled the strike.

November. Eugene A. Schmitz of the Union Labor party
campaigned in the municipal election on a platform to give
labor a larger voice in the affairs of the city. The strike
seemed to provide the necessary sentiment toward Schmitz,
and he was elected along with several other union candidates.
Schmitz, and attorney Abe Ruef, ushered in a new period of
municipal corruption.

1902   The California Historical Landmarks League was organized
            at San Francisco.

            The city became lighted by electricity.

1903   Gentleman James J. Corbett was knocked out by Jim Jeffries
            in ten rounds for the heavyweight title of the world.

            March 23. The News was founded by E.W. Scripps of the
            Scripps-Howard Newspaper chain.

            May 23. The first transcontinental automobile trip was
            made from San Francisco to New York by Dr. H. Nelson
            Jackson and Sewell Crocker.

            November. Mayor Schmitz was re-elected.

1904   October 17. The formation of the Bank of Italy, later re-
            named Bank of America by Amadeo Peter Giannini, became
            the largest private bank in the world.

1905   The University of California purchased the Bancroft Collec-
            tion and moved it to the Berkeley campus where it has since
            tripled.

            The Pacific Gas and Electric Company gained control of al-
            most all the gas, light, and power companies in the San
            Francisco area, and became a public utilities monopoly.

            November. Mayor Schmitz was again re-elected and car-
            ried almost his entire slate of candidates. He defeated re-
            form candidate John Partride, who ran on the Democratic
            ticket.

THE EARTHQUAKE AND RECONSTRUCTION
1906-1920

1906   April 18: 5:13 A.M. San Francisco felt the first shocks of

the greatest earthquake in the city's history; the famous
quake and fire which devastated the city. It was caused by
the cooling and contraction of earth from Point Arena above
Point Reyes, through Bolinas, a part of the San Andreas
fault.

April 18: mid-morning. Fires, caused by overturned wood
stoves, damaged electrical connections, and gas leaks
started in many parts of the city. The fire-alarm system
was out of commission, and the fire chief was killed by the
collapse of a building. The water supply failed, the blaze
was out of control, and devastation was assured.

April 18: noon. Fire spread all over the city. Mayor
Schmitz and the city's leaders formed the Committee of
Fifty to cope with the earthquake and fire. They became the
governing body of the city during the crisis.

The mayor issued a proclamation which ordered: the police
to kill all looters, the gas and lighting companies to turn
off their facilities, a curfew from dusk until dawn, and
warned all citizens of the danger of fire.

To prevent looting and help the firemen, federal troops
were called out. By the end of the day 1,700 soldiers were
on duty. In addition to the regular army, the National Guard
was mobilized, and a citizen's vigilance committee was organized. These forces shot nine people accused of looting.

April 18-19. Houses along Jackson and O'Farrell streets
were blown up to stop the fire, but it was out of control.

General Funston declared martial law, and took charge of
the city.

April 19. Secretary of War Taft directed the Army to send
all needed supplies for the homeless into the city.

April 20. All remaining food in the city was taken over by
the Committee of Fifty, and food rationing was imposed.

Food arrived from army posts and neighboring communities.

April 21. The flames were brought under control. The effects of the disaster were: 4.7 square miles burned; 28,188
buildings destroyed; 311 dead; six shot for crimes; one killed

by mistake; 252 reported missing or unaccounted for; $175,000,000 in claims filed with the insurance companies, all but $8,000,000 of which was paid, and a total property loss estimated at one-half billion dollars.

June 13. Mayor Schmitz and political boss Ruef were arrested following an investigation instigated by ex-Mayor Phelan and a group of reform-minded citizens.

Summer. Reconstruction of the city started, financed in part by insurance money. This caused a building boom in the city.

Laws of the city were revised to try and prevent another such disaster. Building codes were strengthened to insure construction of fire-proof buildings, the fire department was reorganized, new equipment was purchased, and steps were taken to insure an adequate supply of water.

1907   Alcatraz became the western branch of the United States Military Prison at Fort Leavenworth.

June 13. Mayor Schmitz was found guilty of extortion and sentenced to five years in prison.

June 14. With the mayor in prison, the Board of Supervisors took it upon themselves to appoint Charles Boxton as mayor. Schmitz, who had taken the seals of the city to jail, refused to recognize the new mayor, and continued to conduct the city's business from his prison cell.

July. The electorate made the Reform Party candidate, Edward T. Taylor, mayor. Both Schmitz, with the city seals, and Boxton with the approval of the Board of Supervisors, refused to recognize the duly elected mayor and the city found itself with three mayors, each conducting business.

Boxton agreed to leave City Hall. San Francisco now had two mayors.

August 19. The California State Supreme Court ruled in favor of Taylor. Schmitz returned the seals, leaving one mayor, and the end of that period of municipal cooruption and confusion.

Fall. Bubonic plague appeared, precipitating the largest

rat hunt in history. The hunting of infected rats, combined
with extreme sanitation measures, checked the disease.

1908   January. The appellate court reversed the conviction of
Schmitz, and freed Ruef, who had also been convicted of extortion. This decision was later confirmed by the State Supreme Court.

February. The last plague victim died, but the rat and sanitation campaign continued.

Ruef was later rearrested and tried for bribing a supervisor
to vote for a streetcar franchise. During the trial the pro-
secutor, Heney, was shot in the courtroom by a juror.
This shocked the population and silenced the critics of the
reform group. Ruef was reconvicted.

1909   The Tong War broke out in Chinatown.

The Pacific Ocean Exposition Company was formed to make
San Francisco the site of a fair honoring the completion of
the Panama Canal.

President Taft ordered Army engineers to study San Francisco's water problem.

November. The official end of the plague was announced.
During the epidemic seventy-seven people died, and one
hundred and sixty contracted the disease.

November. Municipal elections were held, and the reform
candidates were defeated, marking the end of the graft tri-
als. P.H. McCarthy was elected mayor, and District Attorney Heney was defeated.

1910   The population of the city was 406,912.

January. Voters approved a bond issue of $45,000,000 to
start the Sierra water project. It was the largest publicly
financed enterprise yet undertaken by the city.

April 10. The city supported the coming Panama Exposition
by subscribing to more than $4,000,000 in bonds, and form-
ing groups to put pressure on the federal government to select San Francisco as the site.

1911   Voters approved a plan to purchase the Geary Street Rail-
                road, and the city became the first in America to own and
                operate its own street transportation system.

                January 31. Congress passed a resolution which named San
                Francisco the exposition city, and asked President Taft to
                invite the nations of the world to participate.

                November 11. James Rolph, Jr., was elected mayor and
                continued in office until 1930.

1912   The Board of Supervisors ordered all cemeteries within the
                city limits vacated to make room for the living. This al-
                lowed further expansion of the city.

                The city converted the Geary Street Railroad to an electric
                trolley line and eliminated the old cable cars.

                The city started to prepare a 635 acre site for the coming
                exposition. They filled in the tidelands on the bay between
                Fort Mason and the Golden Gate.

                A bond issue of $8,800,000 authorized construction of the
                civic center. This was the effect of years of discussion on
                the rejected so-called Burnham plan to beautify the city.

                May. Judge Frank H. Dunne dismissed all graft cases,
                (one hundred), before his court. The District Court of Ap-
                peals then ordered the lower court to dismiss the eighty-
                eight remaining indictments against Ruef.

                Schmitz was tried again and acquitted. The reform move-
                ment ended.

                December 8. The first municipally owned railroad began
                operation.

1913   A bond issue for $3,500,000 was approved to extend the
                Geary Street line from Thirty-ninth Avenue to the ocean and
                provide service for the upcoming Panama Exposition.

                The city attempted to purchase all remaining private street
                railroads. They laid parallel tracks on Market Street after
                their offer was refused, and proceeded to put the Market
                Street line out of business by running a city car whenever
                the line ran a car.

April 5. Construction was started on City Hall.

December. President Wilson signed the Riker Act which
legalized San Francisco's request to obtain water from the
Sierras. This broke the deadlock which had existed since
the area was first surveyed in 1901.

1914   The Civic Auditorium was constructed in conjunction with
the Panama Pacific Exposition at a cost of $1,350,000.
Among other things, it contains the largest pipe organ in
the world.

The city gained control of the Hetch Hetchy watershed near
Yosemite which eventually supplied 400,000,000 gallons of
water per day to the city.

1915   February 20. The Panama Pacific Exposition opened to celebrate the completion of the Panama Canal. This was important because it gave impetus to city planning programs
and improvement in the entire San Francisco Bay region.

December 28. The new city hall was dedicated. It cost
$3,500,000 and contained a 308 foot dome, 16 foot, 3 inches
higher than the dome on the Capital at Washington, D.C.

1916   Father John W. Sullivan started restoration of the Mission
Dolores. This was a landmark in the movement to restore
the Spanish heritage of the city.

June 1. The first unified West Coast strike of waterfront
workers began. Four thousand men walked off the job causing another period of labor unrest in the city. The culinary
trades, tugboat crewmen, and structural steel workers also
struck.

July 10. Businessmen and industrialists formed the Law and
Order Committee to bring permanent industrial peace to the
city. Their primary objective was to adopt an open shop
policy, and to replace striking employees with non-union
workers.

July 22. During a preparedness day parade, labor-management violence broke out. A bomb exploded, ten people were
killed and forty were injured.

November 22. The Board of Supervisors adopted an ordinance prohibiting picketing of any business where strike-breakers were employed.

1917   The Twin Peaks Tunnel, which connected the center of the city with outlying regions, was completed. This helped to expand and develop new residential districts. The tunnels were used exclusively by street cars.

The public library was completed at a cost of $1,152,067, including $275,897 from the Carnegie Foundation.

A state-wide red light abatement law was enacted. The law revoked the license of the Barbary Coast dance halls, and was designed to end legalized prostitution.

January 15. Mayor Rolph started his campaign to "clean up vice" in San Francisco.

April 17. The United States entered the First World War. This caused public projects to be suspended, but brought a new prosperity to the city.

July 26. The Zoning Enabling Act became effective, and marked the beginning of systematic zoning in San Francisco.

December 28. The mayor appointed a commission to survey land utilization in conjunction with the new zoning ordinance.

1918   The Intake Station, the first city owned powerhouse, was completed. The power it produced was used for construction work.

A great flu epidemic broke out in the city. Everyone on the street had to wear a mask, and barrels of Dobells solution were kept on the corners for disinfection.

November. At the urging of President Wilson, Governor William Stevens reduced Mooney's death sentence to life imprisonment. Mooney had been sentenced for his part in the riots on Preparedness Day in 1916, and the case had assumed international importance.

1919   A contract to build the 430 foot high O'Shaughnessy Dam across Hetch Hetchy Canyon in the Sierras was awarded. It was the next step in the movement for municipal ownership of all public utilities.

October 7. A makeshift landing and take-off field at the Presidio was the base for a cross-continental competition among military aviators. Fifteen flyers left for New York, while a similar group flew from the east.

THE 1920s

1920   The population of the city reached 506,676.

January 13. So-called radical leaders were arrested as part of the country-wide red scare, and city concern with communist influence in labor unions.

January 16. The 18th Amendment became effective, prohibiting sale of any alcoholic beverage containing more than .5% alcohol. This caused economic problems in the wine country to the north, and to related city businesses.

May 12. The Seventh Annual Foreign Trade Convention was held in San Francisco. This symbolized the importance of the five billion dollar a year foreign commerce enjoyed by the city.

1921   Attempted purchase of the Spring Valley Water Company was part of a plan to bring all public utilities under city control. The voters would not approve the plan.

The Federal Road Act was passed. This brought money and talent to cope with the growing traffic problem in San Francisco. More than a million vehicles in California strained the roads, and this was the start of an efficient highway system which linked the city to the rest of the state and country.

October 7. The War Department began hearings to consider a trans-bay bridge.

Fall. A strike in the building trades brought about organization of an Industrial Association to prevent and settle the many strikes. The strike was settled by disciplining employers and unions alike. This system was adopted by many cities in the country.

1922   March 1. The San Francisco Chamber of Commerce went on record as favoring modification of the Volstead Act. They wanted to permit the sale of beer and light wines.

August 22. A Tong War erupted in Chinatown and police swept the area trying to arrest the leaders.

1923   The State Legislature created the Golden Gate Bridge and
                Highway District which facilitated construction of the bridge.

                January 23. Mae Ella Hunt Logan became the first Con-
                gresswoman from California. She filled her husband's un-
                expired term and was re-elected in the following election.

                April 4. The San Francisco Opera Association was formed.

                Fall. The Commonwealth Club started a regional planning
                organization for the entire bay district. They drew up plans
                to solve the water, food, sewerage, transportation, high-
                way, bridge, port zoning, and conservation problems.
                Their only tangible result was to focus attention on city plan-
                ning and they folded in 1928. Most of their recommendations
                were put into practice at a later date.

1925   The Moccasin Creek power plant which developed 100,000
                horsepower was completed.

                W. A. Bechtel Co., builder of dams, bay bridges, water
                supply systems in the city, and the west, was formed.

1926   Januar 7. Tremors of an earthquake were felt in the city.

                January 26. The U.S. Post Office awarded contracts to de-
                liver airmail to private individuals, and the city started to
                search for a municipal airport site.

                April 1. The Brotherhood of Carpenters and Joiners struck,
                causing labor violence and the arrest of the vice-president
                of the union. Popular sentiment was against the union and
                they lost. Their loss signified lack of union strength in the
                city.

                June 20. The War Department gave its approval to build a
                bridge across the bay.

                October 25. Another earthquake was felt in the city, caus-
                ing only slight damage.

                December 3. The Mark Hopkins Hotel opened at a coast of
                $5,000,000.

1927   January 15. The mile-long Dumbarton Bridge opened. It
                was the first bridge to carry automobile traffic across the

the bay and shortened travel between Alameda County and
San Francisco.

May 7. Mayor Rolph dedicated Mills Field, site for the
municipal airport.

1928
Work started on a highway connecting Dumbarton Bridge
and the city. An underpass beneath the Southern Pacific
tracks in south San Francisco was completed, but the road
was not linked together until February, 1929.

July 1. After a meteorological survey, the U.S. Weather
Bureau recommended the Mills Field site for the airport.

November. Herbert Hoover was elected president. This
was important because, as a native of California, he was
sympathetic to the bay bridge and helped break the legislative block to that project.

November. Voters defeated a $1,700,000 bond issue to con-
vert Mills Field into an airport.

DEPRESSION AND RECOVERY 1929-1941

1929
May 7. The State Legislature created the California Toll
Bridge Authority to facilitate construction of the Oakland
and Golden Gate Bridge. The bridge thus became the joint
responsibility of the state and the city.

October 20. The Bayshore Highway from San Francisco to
San Mateo was dedicated. The construction of highways increased tourism in the area.

1930
The Bank of Italy changed its name to the Bank of America.

San Francisco College for Women was founded.

February 18. Man-made Treasure Island was completed.
The former shoals were raised from a depth of twenty feet
below sea level to an elevation of thirteen feet above mean
low water. When finished its area was 400 acres.

March 3. After approval of a $41,000,000 bond issue, the
city took over the Spring Valley Water Company.

August. The Mills Estate, 1,112.5 acres of land, was pur-

chased at a cost of $1,050,000 for use as a municipal air-
port. Almost half of the land was on the west side of the
Bayshore Highway and could not be used for the airport.

November 6. The California Toll Bridge Authority authorized construction of the bridge. It was financed by state
funds of $6,600,000, and the Reconstruction Finance Cor-
poration purchased bonds totaling $77,200,000, which were
to be repaid with tolls.

1931   The new city charter was passed.

1932   The War Memorial group of buildings, including the War
Memorial Building and the Opera House were completed.

January 8. The new and present city charter became effective.

October 15. The San Francisco Opera House opened with
a performance of La Tosca. Its 3,286 seats and twenty-
five boxes were filled.

1933   Alcatraz Island was turned over to the Department of Justice
by the Army to be used as a federal prison.

The Public Health Building was completed.

The San Francisco Ballet Company was founded to supply
talent for the opera.

January 4. Construction started on the Golden Gate Bridge.

1934   There were many strikes; 561 between October, 1934, and
November, 1936. A new red scare was one of the results.

May 9. Twelve thousand longshoremen walked off the job
in San Francisco and traffic in the port ceased. Later, the
Maritime Union, the Industrial Union, the International Sea-
men's Union, and others joined the strike. It was the worst
strike in the city's history.

July 3. The Industrial Association attempted to break the
strike and violence erupted. Two strikers were shot, nine
policemen, and thirteen citizens were injured.

July 5. Rioting broke out due to the strike.

The National Guard was called out to stop street fighting and restore order.

July 14. The Teamsters' Union joined the strike.

July 16. Most of San Francisco's labor unions struck in sympathy and the city was paralyzed.

July 18. Two hundred people were arrested and accused of being communists and professional agitators.

July 20. The strike ended when the strikers and employers accepted the proposals of the President's Mediation Board.

October 24. The first part of the Hetch Hetchy water supply system was opened. This culminated a thirty-three year battle to obtain an adequate water supply for the city.

1935

The San Francisco Museum of Art opened, confirming the fact that San Francisco was second only to New York as a progressive art center.

City College of San Francisco was founded.

May. Congress passed the Emergency Relief Act which provided money for projects in the Bay area. A large portion of the funds was used to construct harbor defenses and military posts to protect this major west coast port. This allowed San Francisco to fare better than many cities during the depression, and inadvertently prepared the United States for World War II.

1936

San Francisco started to recover from the depression due to $29,000,000 of Federal funds, and the W.P.A. finding employment for 21,500 people.

November 17. President Roosevelt issued a proclamation inviting all nations to attend the opening of the Golden Gate International Exposition.

San Francisco-Oakland Bay Bridge was opened to vehicular traffic. It took three years, four months, and three days to build.

1937

The War Department created a military reservation on the Golden Gate Headlands.

May 27. The Golden Gate Bridge was opened to foot traffic.

May 28. The Golden Gate Bridge was opened to automobiles.

1938 October 4. The California Historical Society met at the Mission Dolores signifying the restoration of that landmark. This was part of the program to revive the Spanish heritage.

1939 Gas lighting of the city streets was entirely abandoned by the end of the year.

The State Legislature granted full power to the highway commission to designate routes for freeways and obtain the land. This was another step in the construction of a modern highway system which linked San Francisco with other major cities, and replaced the railroad as the major form of transportation.

January. Governor Culbert L. Olson, first democratic governor since the turn of the century, pardoned the men imprisoned for the bombing during the Preparedness Day parade of 1916. This culminated twenty-three years of agitation on the part of civil liberty spokesmen.

January 15. Train service between Oakland and San Francisco, via the bridge, started.

February 18. The 1939-1940 Golden Gate International Exposition opened on Treasure Island. The Exposition was held to celebrate the construction of the two bridges.

1940 Treasure Island was leased to the Navy for the duration of the national emergency, and San Francisco started to prepare for the coming war.

December. The Committee to Defend America by Aiding the Allies was formed with headquarters at San Francisco.

WAR AND PEACE 1941-1952

1941 February 28. The Northwestern Pacific Railroad abandoned its inter-urban train and ferry boat service, as it could not compete with motor transportation. The age of the automobile, freeway, and smog had arrived.

The electric train service on the San Francisco-Oakland bridge was also abandoned.

Federal investigators started to examine all San Francisco aliens, mostly the Japanese.

December 7. San Francisco was the first American city to hear of the attack on Pearl Harbor when Admiral Kimmel's famous message, "This is no drill, " was received by the short wave station.

A prisoner of war processing station was opened on Angel Island by the United States Army.

The labor forces at work building military depots and defense establishments in the Bay area numbered 28,000, which created another building boom for the city.

The area quickly became a huge complex of military installations, private shipyards were converted, and work proceeded at the Presidio, Letterman Hostpital, and Forts Mason, Funston, Scott, and Miley.

The number of factories increased by one-third while the number of industrial workers doubled. It was an era of great prosperity, but the lack of transportation, housing, and feeding facilities caused many problems.

1942   Five thousand Japanese citizens, along with several Germans and Italians, were removed from the city and interned by General de Wittalong.

1943   Old "El" cars were brought from New York City to solve a transportation crisis. The crisis was caused by the employment of 269,700 persons in the five counties surrounding San Francisco Bay. The problem became intensified as San Francisco became the major west coast shipping, manufacturing, and embarkation port, as well as the world's largest shipbuilding center. There were also a very large number of servicement in the area.

March 27. Madame Chiang kai-Shek visited Chinatown.

June 12. John McLaren, the planner of Golden Gate Park died. He had planted over a million trees in his lifetime, and due to his influence, the Park contained greater varieties of trees, shrubs, and plants than any other.

1944   By the end of this year the Bay area had received over four billion dollars in war supply contracts.

San Francisco ranked second among the nation's cities as a banking center.

April 3. The U.S. Government acquired title to Treasure Island and a lease on the airport. In return for these concessions the government agreed to give the city over $10,000,000 worth of government constructed facilities at the airport when the war was over.

April 6. The San Francisco Chamber of Commerce started a campaign for unified Bay planning in the postwar period.

1945 A freeway was planned to connect San Francisco with Los Angeles.

Mayor Lapham appointed a citizens Post War Planning Commission to study the city's present and future needs. The report began a new era of urban planning.

April 25 to June 26. Representatives met at the Opera House to write the charter for the United Nations.

July. The cruiser Indianapolis left San Francisco with the atomic bombs which were dropped on Japan.

August 16. The war ended. A victory celebration ended in rioting and chaos.

1946 There was a rebellion at Alcatraz prison.

1947 Voters approved a bond issue to construct a pipeline across San Joaquin Valley. It was completed in 1950, and brought in an additional 76,000,000 gallons of water daily.

1950 The population was 775,551.

The population started to decline as the land for new building ran out, and there was a sharp rise in real estate prices.

Some U.C.L.A. professors refused to sign a loyalty oath and this caused a campus disruption. It was part of the postwar red scare. Seven members of San Francisco State College and two nonacademic employees were fired for failing to sign the loyalty oath.

Shipping tonnage in the port fell 194,618 tons behind Los Angeles.

The Board of Supervisors refused to abide by the Fair Employment Practices Law.

August 5. Harry Bridges, president of the Longshoremen's Union, was convicted of perjury and conspiracy, and began his jail sentence. The arrest and conviction of Bridges was another symbol of the communist paranoia that the city and the country experienced.

November. A proposition to legalize gambling was defeated. The proposition was important because it showed that San Francisco's boom period was over and the citizens were looking for another way to maintain it.

1951   April 18. General Douglas MacArthur returned to the United States via San Francisco International Airport and was greeted by 3000 people. Two hundred policemen were on duty to keep order.

May 19. The San Francisco Maritime Museum opened.

September 8. President Truman signed the treaty that ended war with Japan at the War Memorial Opera House.

November. Mayor Elmer Robinson was elected, defeating George Christopher.

The Board of Regents of the University of California withdrew their demands that all employees sign a loyalty oath. Thus, a victory for academic freedom was won.

THE MODERN PERIOD 1952-1970

1952   The purchase of the California Street Cable Railroad Company by the city completed municipal control and ownership of all public street transportation.

1953   Plans started for an integrated freeway system to rim the Bay.

1954   The California State Fair was held in San Francisco, and a time capsule was buried to be exhumed one hundred years later.

Nike Ajax guided missiles sites began to replace the anti-aircraft batteries that had defended the city.

1956   August. The Republican National convention that nominated
                Dwight Eisenhower and Richard Nixon met at the Cow Palace.

                November. A $25,000,000 bond issue was approved to build
                a second terminal at the San Francisco International Airport,
                and lengthen the runways to accomodate jet liners.

1957   The New York Giants migrated to Seals Stadium and later
                to Candlestick Park, which was owned by the San Francisco
                Park and Recreation Committee.

                The Richomond-San Rafael Bridge which spanned the north-
                ern arm of the Bay was completed.

1958   The Eastshore Freeway was opened from San Francisco to
                San Jose, and was named the Chester M. Nimitz Freeway
                after the naval hero.

                The Carquinez Bridge was completed across the Bay.

                The San Francisco Ballet Company left on a world tour, be-
                coming the first American classical ballet company to do
                so.

1959   The Crown Zelerback Building on Bush Street opened.

1960   The population reached 742,855.

                The Cherry River powerhouse, which cost $30,000,000 and
                had a capacity of 187,000 horsepower, was completed.

                December. The Army disposed of 291 acres from its Gol-
                den Gate Reservation, recognizing the new age of defense
                for that region.

1961   The San Francisco and Oakland Helicopter Airlines started
                to service the Bay area.

                The City Planning Commission proposed a massive urban
                renewal for the city to solve the postwar problems, which
                included slums, transportation, housing, loss of business
                and population. They also suggested unified planning for all
                Bay communities.

                October. The voters approved a $115,000,000 bond issue,
                which was the largest in history, in order to increase the
                water supply again.

1962   October. The <u>San Francisco Examiner</u> combined with the
            <u>Bulletin</u> and the <u>News Call</u>; the merger reflected the declin-
            ing status of the newspaper industry in the television age.

            November 6. Residents of San Francisco and other counties
            voted in favor of a rapid transit system to link the Bay com-
            munities. A gond issue of $793,000,000 was passed to fi-
            nance the project.

1963   A suggestion to place a nuclear power plant at Bodega Bay,
            north of San Francisco, aroused great controversy and was
            delayed.

            July. Blacks in San Francisco demanded an open occupancy
            policy in housing. This was important because it showed
            that by the 1960's blacks were becoming an important minor-
            ity in the city.

1964   January 1. J.F. Shelley became the first Democratic mayor
            of the city in fifty-five years.

            Summer. The Republican National Convention which nomi-
            nated Barry Goldwater was held in San Francisco.

            September 14. The age of campus unrest began at Berkeley
            when the Dean of Students prohibited students from soliciting
            funds for the presidential campaign. A United Front ap-
            peared to oppose the University's actions. The United
            Front later became the Free Speech movement.

            October 1. A mob of 2,000 students formed at the Univer-
            sity to protest and prevent the arrest of Jack Weinberg, who
            had been active in the demonstrations.

            October 3. The students organized the Free Speech Move-
            ment.

            December 2. Members of the Free Speech Movement occu-
            pied the University for a sit-in.

            Governor Edmund Brown ordered the police onto the campus.

            December 3. Police arrested 814 demonstrators, but the
            demonstrations continued. The President and Chancellor
            of the University resigned.

The demonstrations ended.

1965   The hippie movement flourished in the Haight-Ashbury district near Golden Gate Park. San Francisco, with its usual permissiveness, accepted the flower children. This community, along with the East Village in New York City, became the center of the new counter-culture.

The Bay Area Rapid Transit System started construction.

April. An urban planning study noted that the city needed at least $45,000,000 in urban renewal probrams to stop the loss of population, which was, percentage wise, larger than any other American city.

1966   The Diamond Heights urban renewal project, close to the geographical center of the city, neared completion. The former wastelands were converted into a community that would provide housing for 2,427 families.

1966   January. At the San Francisco Tripps Festival a new musical form was proclaimed; acid-rock. San Francisco became the capital of the music industry with this new sound, producing such stars as Janis Joplin, The Grateful Dead, Big Brother and the Holding Company.

1967   Violence mounted in the city due to the influx of the drug culture. The Haight-Ashbury district started to deteriorate and turn into a slum.

Work started on the Golden Gateway project in a former wholesale produce district which had been reclaimed from the Bay in the middle of the nineteenth century. The plan called for eight 22-story apartment houses, 140 residences, and a commercial area dominated by a 25-story office building and other services.

The Japanese Cultural Center was completed. It was the first of its kind in the United States, and a far cry from the old days of racial prejudices.

May 5. Anti-war agitation broke out in the city.

November. J.L. Allioto was elected mayor.

A proposal to withdraw from Viet Nam was defeated by the voters.

1968   February 14. The $15,000,000 Japanese Center was dedi-
                cated with Shinto rites.

                November. One hundred black militants protested racial
                policies at San Francisco State College. A demonstration
                started which led to a student strike.

                November 7. Police were called in and the college closed.

                November 15. Governor Reagan protested the actions of
                the university in closing.

                December 3. Classes resumed with police protection, but
                the distrubances continued.

                December 5. Police were called onto the campus, and used
                mace on the striking students.

1969   March 21. The Student strike at San Francisco State College
                ended.

                May 15. The Battle of Berkeley occurred. Hippies were
                using land that the University wanted to convert into new
                buildings. Six thousand students attended a rally on campus,
                and violence erupted when the police confronted the students;
                one student died, one was blinded, and many were shot.

                The Circuit Court enjoined the sheriff to have his men stop
                beating the students taken prisoner during the riots.

                Governor Reagan declared a state of emergency and called
                out the National Guard.

                May 21. Helicopters sprayed gas on the campus and the
                riot ended.

                June 29. The city planned a $200,000,000 sports complex.

                September 23. Mayor Allioto was accused by Look maga-
                zine of ties with the Cosa Nostra. He denied the charges
                and filed a $12,500,000 libel suit against the magazine.

1970   February 17. The San Francisco police station was bombed
                by agitators.

                February 18. Mayor Allioto offered $5,000 reward for the
                capture of, or information about, the bombers.

March 14. Municipal employees went out on strike for the first time in the city's history, paralyzing the city.

March 16. The municipal employees' strike ended.

DOCUMENTS

This section presents as wide a variety of primary documents concerned with the growth and development of San Francisco as possible in a short volume such as this. It contains city charters, ordinances, contemporary accounts and descriptions, and newspaper commentary. The documents were culled from a number of different sources, and give a comprehensive picture of San Francisco's history. Obviously, much more could have been included, but what follows will give the interested student a good starting point for further study into the documentary materials concerned with this complex and fascinating metropolis.

THE DISCOVERY OF SAN FRANCISCO BAY, 1774

The actual discovery of San Francisco Bay was made by the exploration party of Gaspar de Portola. They were trying to find a good harbor that would lend itself to settlement and thus check Russian expansion from the north. The following is a record of the first sighting of the Bay from the diary of Father Crespi, who accompanied the expedition.

(Source: Bolton, Herbert Eugene, Anza's California Expedition, Berkeley, 1930.)

To-day, All Soul's Day, we two celebrated Mass for the souls in Purgatory, and after Mass some of the soldiers asked permission to go out to hunt, for many deer have been seen. Some of them went quite a distance from camp and climbed the hills, so that it was already night when they returned. They said that toward the north they had seen an immense arm of the sea, or an estuary, which penetrated into the land as far as an eye could reach, extending to the southeast; that they had seen some beautiful plains well adorned with trees, and that the smokes which they saw in all directions left no doubt that the country was thickly populated with heathen villages. This report comfirmed us still more in the opinion that we were on the port of Our Father San Francisco, and that the arm of the sea which they told us about was certainly the estuary of which the pilot Cabrera Bueno spoke.

THE FOUNDING OF SAN FRANCISCO, 1776

In 1776 Juan Bautista de Anza was sent from Mexico to form a colony at San Francisco Bay. Father Palou, who accompanied Anza, described the founding of the Presidio and of the Mission San Francisco, later renamed the Mission Dolores.

(Source: Bolton, Herbert Eugene, Anza's California Expedition Berkeley, 1930.)

It has already been said that by order of Commander Rivera twelve of the soldiers who had come with the expedition of Senor Anza had remained at San Gabriel and their families with them; and it has also been noted that the same commander sent an order for them to go up to Monterey. This was done and they arrived at that presidio on the 28th day of May. . . .

In a few days the San Carlos dropped anchor at Monterey, and its commander, as has been said, dispatched a courier to San Diego. While awaiting the reply he unloaded what belonged to the presidio, and in its place he put what was destined for the presidio of San Francisco. Not having any reason to delay, the lieutenant set out with his expedition. . . .

On the 17th day of June, 1776, about two in the afternoon, the company of soldiers and families from Sonora set out from Monterey. It was composed of its commander Lieutenant Don Jose Joaquin Moraga, a sergeant, two corporals, and ten soldiers, all with their wives and families except the commander, who had left his in Sonora. In addition there were seven families of settlers, rationed and provisioned by the king; other persons attached to the soldiers and their families; five servant boys, muleteers and vaqueros, who conducted about two hundred of the king's cattle and some belonging to individuals, and the mule train which carried the provisions and utensils necessary for the road. All of the foregoing belonged to the new presidio. And for whatever concerned the first mission that was to be founded we two ministers, Father Fray Pedro Benito Cambon and I, went with two servants who conducted the loads, and three unmarried Indian neophytes, two of them from Old California and the other from the mission of Carmelo, who drove the cattle for the mission, numbering eighty-six head, which were incorporated with those for the presidio.

The officers of the vessels, with their pilots and chaplains, wished to accompany the expedition, and they all did so for about half a league. From this point the captain of the Principe and all the pilots turned back; but Don Fernando Quiros continued for the first day's march with the two father chaplains as far as the Monterey River, where the expedition halted and comped. On the following day, after having watched all the people cross the river and seen the line formed on that broad plain by all those people, the pack trains, cattle, and the horse herd, they returned to Monterey after taking farewell in the hope that we would soon meet in the port of Our Father San Francisco.

The expedition continued by the same road which was traveled in
the exploration of that harbor in the year 1774. . . .But the day's marches
were shorter, in order not to fatigue the little children and the women,
especially those who were pregnant, and for this reason it was even
necessary to make several stops. On the whole way there was not a single
mishap, thanks to God. We were well received by all the heathen whom we
met on the road, who were surprised to see so many people of both sexes
and all ages, for up to that time they had not seen more than some few
soldiers, on the occasions when they went to make the explorations. And
they were astonished at the cattle, which they had never seen before.

On the 27th day of June the expedition arrived in the neighborhood
of the harbor, and the commander ordered the camp halted on the bank of
a lagoon called by Senor Anza Nuestra Senora de los Dolores, which is
in sight of the bay of Los Llorones (Mission Bay) and the beach of the bay
or arm of the sea which runs to the southeast, with the intention of waiting
here for the bark in order to select the spot for the founding of the fort
and presidio, and in the meantime to explore the land. On the following
day he ordered a shelter of branches built to serve as a chapel in which
to celebrate the holy sacrifice or Mass. In it the first Mass was said on
the 29th, the feast of the great, holy apostles, San Pedro and San Pablo,
and we continued to celebrate in it every day until the camp was moved
to the site which it occupies near the landing place, when the ground and the
convenience of water permitted it.

As soon as the expedition halted, the heathen of the surrounding
villages come to the camp, attracted by the novelty of seeing such neighbors
in their country. They came to visit us frequently, bringing their rude
gifts of mussels and wild seeds, which were always reciprocated with beads
and some of our food, to which they soon took a liking, except the milk,
which they refused to taste.

These natives are well formed, many of them being bearded, bald,
and rather homely, for they have a habit of pulling out the hair of their
eyebrows by the roots, which makes them ugly. They are poor, and have
no houses except little enclosures made of brush to shelter them somewhat
from the heavy winds which prevail and are extremely annoying. The men
go totally naked, though here and there one covers his shoulders with a
sort of a little cape of beaver skins and pelican feathers. The women cover
themselves only with plaited tules, for very few skins of animals are seen
among them.

For an entire month the expedition remained in that camp, which was
composed of field tents, waiting for the bark. Meanwhile soldiers, citizens,
and servants employed themselves in cutting logs in order to have this done
when the bark should arrive. The lieutenant busied himself in exploring
the land in the vicinity, where he found some springs of water, lagoons,
pastures, and good sites for all kinds of stock. Near the white cliff he
found two springs of water sufficient for the use of the presidio, and not
far from them he found a good plain which is in view of the harbor and
entrance, and also of its interior. As soon as he saw the spot the lieutenant
decided that it was suitable for the presidio but he delayed moving the
people there, as he was awaiting day by day for the arrival of the packet.

Seeing that it did not appear for a whole month, and as they wrote from Monterey by the pack train which went to bring provisions, that it had sailed long ago, the lieutenant decided to move to that spot so that the soldiers might begin to build their huts for shelter, since it was nearer at hand for making a beginning of the houses. This he did on the 26th of July, setting to work immediately to construct some tule huts. The first was the one that was to serve as a chapel, and in it I said Mass on the 28th of the same month.

Notwithstanding that the order of the commander, which was sent from San Diego to the lieutenant, was to found the presidio only, yet, seeing that he had plenty of men, among soldiers and settlers; that the site of the first mission was so near the presidio; and that as far as he had observed the heathen in the vicinity there was no reason at that time to fear them, as they had shown signs of friendship, the lieutenant decided that we two missionaries should remain, with a guard of six soldiers, all the cattle, and the other things belonging to the mission, so that hand might be put to cutting timbers for a dwelling; and he charged the soldiers and one settler to do the same, so as to have a place to live in with their families. . . .

As soon as the bark was made fast, the commander, pilots, and Father Nocedal went ashore. When they saw the site of the camp they were all of the opinion that it was a very suitable place for the fort and presidio, and they thought the same of the site of the Laguna de los Dolores for the mission. In view of the opinion of the captain of the bark and the pilots, work was begun on the building of the houses and the presidio. A square measuring ninety-two varas each way was marked out for it, with divisions for church, royal offices, warehouses, guardhouses, and houses for soldier settlers, a map of the plan being formed and drawn by the firs pilot.

And so that the work might be done as speedily as possible, the commander designated a squad of sailors and the two carpenters to join the servants of the royal presidio in making a good warehouse in which to keep the provisions, a house for the commanding officer of the presidio, and a chapel for celebrating the holy sacrifice of the Mass, while the soldiers were making their own houses for their families.

The work of the presidio being now under way, Captain Don Fernando Quiros came to the site of the mission, accompanied by the chaplain, a pilot, the surgeon, and six sailors, to aid in building a church or chapel in which to celebrate Mass and a room to live in. With this assistance the buildings were begun, and everything progressed so well that by the middle of September the soldiers had their houses already made of logs, all with flat roofs; the lieutenant had his government house, and a warehouse of the same material was finished large enough to store all the provisions brought by the bark.

It was then decided that the formal act of possession should take place, the day appointed for it being that on which our Mother Church celebrates the impression of the stigmata of Our Seraphic Father San Francisco, that is, the 17th of September, a most appropriate day, since he is the patron of the harbor, the new presidio, and the mission. And for taking formal possession of the mission the 4th of October was designated, which is the day dedicated to Our Seraphic Father San Francisco. . . .

It has already been said that notwithstanding the order of Commander

Don Fernando Rivera that for the present the presidio alone should
be founded, his lieutenant decided that the founding might go on, for
he had enough men for both the presidio and a mission. With this object,
when the expedition set out to make a beginning of the buildings of the
presidio, he left us two missionaries in this place at the Laguna de los
Dolores, with an escort of six soldiers, one named as corporal in command, and a citizen settler with his family, besides the families of the
six soldiers, who were married. As soon as we found ourselves alone
work was begun, aided by the three servants, in cutting timber to begin
the building of the chapel and the dwelling houses. By the time the bark
arrived we already had plenty of timber, and with the aid of some
sailors, who were furnished by Commander Quiros, in a short time a
house ten varas long and five wide, all of wood, covered with clay and
with a roof of tule, was finished. Immediately afterward a church, eighteen
varas long, was built of the same material, with a room for the sacristy
behind the altar, and adorned as well as possible with cloths and drapery
and with the banners and pennants of the bark. The chapel was blessed
with all ceremony on the 3d of October, the eve of the Feast of Our
Seraphic Father, it being our intention to celebrate the occasion on the
following day with due solemnity. But, as the lieutenant had not returned
from his expedition at the end of the day, it was agreed to postpone the
founding and merely to sing a Mass on the day of Our Seraphic Father,
as was done.

On the 8th of the same month, the lieutenant having arrived the
previous afternoon, the ceremony was performed, in the presence of the
gentlemen of the bark and all the crew except those required to take
care of the vessel, and of the commander of the presidio with all the
troops and citizens, only those that were absolutely required remaining
at the fort. I sang the Mass with the ministers, and at its conclusion a
procession was formed, in which an image of Our Seraphic Father San
Francisco, patron of the port, presidio, and mission, was carried on a
frame. The function was celebrated with repeated salvos of muskets,
rifles, and the swivel guns that were brought from the bark for the purpose, and also with rockets. All the people who were present at the
ceremony remained at the mission to dine, two beeves having been killed for
their entertainment. In the afternoon the men returned to the presidio
and the crew went on board, the day having been a very joyous one for
all. The only ones who did not enjoy this happy day were the heathen, as
I shall relate at length in the next chapter.

The founding of the presidio and mission concluded, the sea commander decided to prepare the bark for its return to San Blas, ordering
wood and water taken on and the necessary ballast loaded. Everything
being finished, and the weather favorable, it safely left this harbor on the
morning of the 21st of October.

The successful founding of the mission had been greatly promoted
not only by the presence of the gentlemen at the function, but also by
the aid of some sailors, who assisted in the building, and of the carpenter, who made the doors of the church and the house, and a table with
two drawers for the altar. Besides this, a gift was made of a cayuco
and a net for fishing. At the same time it was arranged that four sailors

should remain as laborers, completing the number of six who were allowed by his Excellency. With this reinforcemnt the work proceeded on the buildings and in preparing the land for planting. Crops were put in and a good stream of water for irrgating was conducted by a ditch which passes close to the houses. . . .

DESCRIPTION OF CONDITIONS IN SAN FRANCISCO, 1816

The reason for the existence of the San Francisco garrison was to protect the Spanish American frontier from other countries. The colony was never well supplied, nor were the fortifications very formidable, a fact noticed and observed by a Russian visit in 1816. It was published reports like this that encouraged the Russians, British, and later the Americans to consider the possibility of separating the colony from Spain.

(Source: Chamisso, Adelbert von, A Sojourn at San Francisco Bay in 1816, San Francisco, 1936.)

The Captain here, as in Chile, succeeded in making the Commandant and his officers familiar guests at our table. We ate on shore, in the tent, and our friends at the Presidio were always promptly on hand. This condition of things arose spontaneously. The misery in which they languished, forgotten and deserted for six or seven years by Mexico, their mother-land, did not permit them to be hosts; and the need felt to pour out their hearts to some one, drove them to us, with whom they live easily and comfortably. They spoke with bitterness of the missionaries, who, with all the lack of provisions, yet lived, having abundance of the produce of the earth. Now that their money was spent, the missionaries would deliver to them nothing without a requisition, and even then only that which was absolutely indispensable to their sustenance; this not including bread or meal; so that for years, without seeing bread, they lived on maize. Even the garrisons, which were in all the missions, for their protection, were provided with necessities only upon requisition. "Los Senores are too good," exclaimed Don Miguel (meaning the commandants); "they should insist on supplies." A soldier went further, and complained to us that the commandant would not permit them to press natives from the opposite shore, in order to force them to work for the soldiers, as they did in the missions.

Discontents arose, also, because the new governor of Monterey, Don Pablo Vicente de Sola, had, since his entry upon the duties of his office, set himself in opposition to smuggling, which alone had provided them with the indispensable necessaries. . . .

DESCRIPTION OF SAN FRANCISCO BY THE RUSSIAN EXPLORER OTTO VON KOTZEBUE, 1824

Eight years later, another Russian ship tested the Spanish defenses. In the following document, the Russian explorer, Otto von Kotzebue, describes that experience on October 8, 1824.

(Source: Kotzebue, Otto von, A New Voyage Round the World, in the Years, 1823, 24, and 26, London, 1830.)

The channel leading into the beautiful basin of St. Francisco is only a half gun-shot wide and commanded by a fortress situated on its left bank, on a high rock, named after St. Joaquim. We could distinguish the republican flag, the waving signal, that even this most northern colony of Spain no longer acknowledged the authority of the mother country; we also remarked a few cavalry and a crowd of people who were watching our swiftly sailing vessel with most eager attention. As we drew nearer, a sentinel grasped with both hands a long speaking trumpet, and enquired our nation and from whence we came. This sharp interrogatory, the sight of cannon pointed upon our track, and the military, few indeed, but ready for battle, might have induced an opinion that the fortress had power to refuse entrance even to a ship of war, had we not been acquainted with the true state of affairs. St. Joaquin, on this rocky throne, is, truly a very peaceable and well-disposed saint; no one of his cannon is in condition to fire a single shot, and his troops are cautious in venturing into actual conflict; he fights only with words. As soon as we had dropped anchor, the whole military left the fortress without garrison, to mingle with the assemblage of curious gazers on the shore. . . .

DESCRIPTION OF SAN FRANCISCO BY FREDERICK WILLIAM BEECHEY, 1825

The British also noticed the neglect of the colony and were interested in it in 1825.

(Source: Beechey, Frederick William, Narrative of a Voyage to the Pacific, London, 1856.)

The governor's abode was in a corner of the presidio, and formed one end of a row, of which the other was occupied by a chapel; the opposite side was broken down, and little better than a heap of rubbish and bones, on which jackals, dogs, and vultures were constantly preying; the other two sides of the quadrangle contained storehouses, artificers' shops, and the gaol, all built in the humblest style with badly burnt bricks, and roofed with tiles. The chapel and the governor's house were distinguished by being whitewashed.

Whether viewed at a distance or near, the establishment impresses a spectator with any other sentiment than that of its being a place of authority, and but for a tottering flag-staff, upon which was occasionally displayed the tri-colored flag of Mexico, three rusty field pieces, and a half-accoutred sentinel parading the gateway in charge of a few poor wretches heavily shackled, a visitor would be ignorant of the importance of the place. The neglect of the government to its establishments could not be more thoroughly evinced than in the dilapidated condition of the buildings in question; and such was the dissatisfaction of the people that there was no inclination to improve their condition, or even to remedy many of the evils which they appeared to us to have the power to remove.

The plain upon which the presidio stands is well adapted to cultivation; but it is scarcely ever touched by the plough, and the garrison is entirely beholden to the mission for its resources. Each soldier has nominally about three pounds a month, out of which he is obliged to purchase his provision. If the governor were active, and the means were supplied, the country in the vicinity of the establishment might be made to yield enough wheat and vegetables for the troops, by which they would save that portion of their pay which now goes to the purchase of these necessary articles.

The garrison of San Francisco. . .consists of seventy-six cavalry soldiers and a few artillerymen, distributed between the presidios and the missions, and consequently not more than half a dozen are at any time on one place. They appear to be very dissatisfied. . . .

AN AMERICAN VISIT TO SAN FRANCISCO, 1825

In 1825, an American ship visited San Francisco. Benjamin Morrell, who wrote a narrative of the journey and visit, also noticed the Spanish garrison's state of decay, and mused about the value of that territory to the United States.

(Source: Morrell, Benjamin, Narrative of Four Voyages to the Sea, New York, 1832.)

Were these beautiful regions. . .which are so little known, the property of the United States, our government would never permit them to remain thus neglected. The eastern and middle states would pour out their thousands of emigrants until magnificent cities would rise on the shores of every inlet along the coast of New California, while the wilderness of the interior would be made to blossom like the rose.

SAN FRANCISCO IN 1835

The most widely read of all the books describing San Francisco during the Mexican period was Richard Henry Dana's Two
Years Before the Mast. Dana visited California in 1835, and
wrote the following description. The reader should note the lack
of change and growth during the entire Spanish-Mexican period.

(Source: Richard H. Dana, Two Years Before the Mast, New York
1840.)

About thirty miles from the mouth of the bay, and on the southeast
side, is a high point upon which the presidio is built. Behind this is the
harbor in which trading vessels anchor, and near it, the mission of
San Francisco, and newly begun settlement, mostly of Yankee Californians, called Yerba Buena, which promises well. Here, at anchor, and
the only vessel, was a brig under Russian colors, from Asitka, in Russian
America, which had come down to winter, and to take in a supply of tallow
and grain, great quantities of which latter article are raised in the missions
at the head of the bay. . .

Our anchorage was between a small island, called Yerba Buena, and
a gravel beach in a little bight or cove of the same name, formed by two
small, projecting points. Beyond, to the westward of the land-place, were
dreary sand-hills, with little grass to be seen, and a few trees, and beyond
them higher hills, steep and barren, their sides gullied by the rains.
Some six miles beyond the landing-place, to the right, was a ruinous
Presidio, and some three or four miles to the left was the Mission of
Dolores, as ruinous as the Presidio, almost deserted, with but few
Indians attached to it, and but little property in cattle. Over a region
far beyond our sight there were no other human habitations, except that
an enterprising Yankee, years in advance of his time, had put up, on the
rising ground above the landing, a shanty of rough boards, where he
carried on a very small retail trade between the hide ships and the
Indians. Vast banks of fog, invading us from the North Pacific, drove in
through the entrance, and covered the whole bay; and when they disappeared,
we saw a few well-wooded islands, the sand-hills on the west, the grassy
and wooded slopes on the east, and the vast stretch of the bay to the
southward, where we were told lay the Missions of Santa Clara and San
Jose, and still longer stretches to the northward and northeastward, where
we understood smaller bays spread out, and large rivers poured in their
tributes of waters. There were no settlements on these bays or rivers,
and the few ranchos and Missions were remote and widely separated.
Not only the neighborhood of our anchorage, but the entire region of the
great bay, was solitude. . . . .

DESCRIPTION OF SAN FRANCISCO, 1837

The pitiful state of the city's defenses was noted by Philip Leget Edwards in 1837 when he visited the city. He also makes some philosophical comments about the differences between English and Spanish settlements, and there is a hint of Manifest Destiny in his writing.

(Source: Edwards, Philip Leget, The Diary of Philip Leget Edwards, San Francisco, 1932.)

. . . .The Presidio is a building, the walls of adobes and the roofs of tiles, enclosing a square area, the sides of which are perhaps three hundred feet long. Since the expulsion of the Spaniards in the revolution (of 1821, when Mexico gained its independence from Spain), the place has been going to ruins. One entire side is fallen and parts of the others. All of the outer buildings, of which there were many, are now fallen except one. It is now inhabited by a half dozen families, too indolent to do anything to arrest the progress of decay. A sort of military burlesque is here still supported at times. I found the fort, which once commanded the entrance to the bay in the same ruininous condition. Some of the cannon bore inscriptions dated A.D. 1648. Ruins, however diminutive, are melancholy mementoes of human blindness and folly. These humble ruins, thought I, vie not with those more extensive and magnificent found in the old world, but are equally indicative of debased propensities. I am not gazing upon the ravages of war. These are simply the ravages of time -- of a little time! A little circumspection and industry would have averted all. One American colony, supposing itself aggrieved, has dissolved its connection with its transatlantic parent, and assumed a "separate and equal station" -- has risen to grandeur and happiness; another, without the same causes of complaint, and without the essential qualifications in itself, ventures upon the same experiment, and sinks down into an anarchy more abhorrent than despotism. . . .

THE UNITED STATES TAKES POSESSION OF SAN FRANCISCO, 1846

> On July 9, 1846, the U.S. ship <u>Portsmouth</u>
> entered the harbor and took possession of
> the city without any opposition. An eyewit-
> ness account of that event follows:

(Source: Anonymous. "Filings from an Old Saw," <u>The Golden Era</u>, San
Francisco, 1852.)

The morning of the ninth of July broke bright and beautiful [recalled
"Filings"], and long before the sun rose, the crew of the <u>Portsmouth</u> were
roused from their hammocks, and contrary to usual custom, the decks
were left to their own fate for the nonce, for far more important affairs
were on the <u>tapis</u> than the mere cleaning of decks and scouring of brass.
Breakfast was served at six A.M., and the word passed for all hands to
clean in white frocks, blue pants, black hats and shoes, and prepare for
muster. Breakfast was soon dispatched, for everybody was too much interested in the crowding events of the day to have much appetite, and long before the sound of the drum called us to muster, the boys might be seen each
in his respective station around the guns.

Precisely at eight, the drum beat to quarters, and the captain made
a speech of eleven or eight words, which conveyed to us the idea that he,
in obedience to orders from the commodore should hoist the Stars and
Stripes in the public square that day and take possession in the name of the
United States of America. The first lieutenant then called over a list of
carbineers, who were for the nonce to become soldiers and form a part of
the city detail. The marines under the command of Lieutenant Watson were
in full dress, and every officer of the ship, save two who remained on board
to fire a national salute, were to accompany the party.

As soon as the retreat was beaten, the boats were ordered alongside,
and the marines and carbineers filed into them. We were landed on what
is now Clark's Point, and when all were on shore, formed into sections,
and to the soul-inspiring tune of Yankee Doodle from our band, consisting
of one drum and fife, with an occasional put-in from a stray dog or discon-
solate jackass in the line of march, trudged proudly up through Montgomery
Street to Clay, up Clay to the Plaza, and formed a hollow square. Here
we rested on our arms, while the aides of the commander in chief dissemi-
nated themselves through the town and gathered together some thirty or
forty persons of all nations, colors, and languages, and having penned them
in the square formed by the soldier-sailors, the captain, putting on all his
peculiar dignity, walked up to the flagstaff and gave a majestic nod to his
second in command. The first lieutenant gave a similar nod to one of our
quartermasters, who came forward, flag in hand, and bent it on the halyards.

This was an eventful moment. Something was about to be done that could not be easily undone, and as I gazed upon that crowd of manly faces, I fancied I could read a settled determination to do or die in defense of the act of this day, should it become necessary. Captain M. Montgomery had a proclamation ready prepared, and our first lieutenant now read it to the assembled crowd, and when he finished, gave the signal, and in a moment, amid a roar of cannon from the ship, the hurrahs of the ship's company, the vivas of Californians, the cheers of the Dutchmen, and barking of dogs, the braying of jackasses, and the general confusion of sounds from every living thing within hearing, that flag floated proudly up, which has never yet been lowered to mortal foe. When the ceremony was over and the captain had proclaimed himself governor of the northern portion of Upper California, he constituted Lieutenant Watson of the marines as commander of the town of Yerba Buena, and giving him a garrison consisting of twenty-four rank and file marines, installed him in the adobe custom house, which from thenceforth assumed the name of barracks, and made him at once, from a poor lieutenant of marines, the great and noble potentate of the village. . . .

THE NAMING OF SAN FRANCISCO BY ALCALDE BARTLETT,
January 23, 1847.

>   Under Mexican and Spanish rule, San Francisco
>   was called Yerba Buena, or good herb after the
>   herbs found on the island. After possession of
>   the town passed to the United States, the name
>   was changed to San Francisco by the following
>   order.

(Source: The California Star, January 30, 1847.)

Whereas the local name of Yerba Buena as applied to the settlement
or town of San Francisco, is unknown beyond the immediate district, and
has been applied from the local name of the cove in which the town is built
-- therefore, to prevent confusion and mistakes in the public documents,
and that the town may have the advantage of the name given on the published
maps, it is hereby ordered that the name San Francisco shall hereafter be
used in all official communications and public documents or records apper-
taining to the town.

LETTER FROM COLONEL R.B. MASON TO GEORGE HYDE
July 15, 1847.

> The first government of San Francisco under
> American rule was an alcalde appointed by the
> military governor. This one-man government
> proved unsatisfactory for a growing community.
> Therefore, in the Summer of 1847, the military
> governor of California, Colonel R. B. Mason,
> wrote to the alcalde of San Francisco, George
> Hyde, and directed him to form a town council
> to aid him in administering the settlement.

(Source: The Laws of San Francisco, 1847, San Marino, California, 1847.)

Sir: There is wanted in San Francisco an efficient town government, more so than is in the power of an alcalde alone to put in force. There soon may be expected a large number of whalers in your bay, and a large increase in your population by the arrival of emigrants; it is therefore highly necessary that you should, at an early day, have an efficient town police, proper town laws, town officials & c, for the enforcement of the laws for the preservation of order, and for the proper protection of persons and property.

I therefore desire you to call a town meeting for the election of six persons, who, when elected, shall constitute the town council and who in conjunction with the alcalde, shall constitute the town authorities until the end of the year 1848.

All the municipal laws and regulations will be formed by the council, but executed by the alcalde in his judicial capacity, as at present. The first alcalde will preside at meetings of the council, but shall have no vote, except in cases where the votes are equally divided.

The town council (not less than four of which shall constitute a quorum for the transaction of business), to appoint all necessary town officers, such as treasurer, constables, watchmen, &c., and to determine their pay, fees, &c. The town treasurer to enter into ample and sufficient bonds, conditioned for the faithful performance of his duties, the bonds to be fully, executed to the satisfaction of the council before the treasurer enters upon his duties.

The second alcalde shall, in case of the absence of the first alcalde, take his place and preside at the council, and perform all the proper functions of the first alcalde. No soldier, sailor, or marine, nor any person who is not a "bona fide" resident of the town, shall be allowed to vote for a member of the town council.

THE LAWS OF THE TOWN OF SAN FRANCISCO, 1847

The earlier letter was the sole legal basis for
the acts of the town council of 1847, formed by
an election held on September 13th, of that year.
Under that authority, the council proceeded to
pass a number of laws to govern the growing
community. The laws passed reflect some of
the problems that the town had to contend with
during those early days.

(Source: The Laws of San Francisco, 1847, San Marino, California, 1847.)

TO PREVENT DESERTION OF SEAMEN.

BE IT ORDAINED BY THE TOWN COUNCIL OF THE TOWN OF SAN
FRANCISCO, that if any person within the limits of this Town, shall entice
or advise any Sailor or other person employed on board of any vessel within this harbor or bay, to leave the vessel on which he or they may be employed, upon conviction thereof, shall be fined not exceeding five hundred
dollars, nor less than twenty, and be imprisoned not exceeding three
months.

BE IT FURTHER ORDAINED, that if any person or persons shall
feed, harbor or employ, any runaway Sailor within the limits of this town
without permission from the Alcalde, such person or persons shall be
fined on conviction thereof, not exceeding five hundred dollars, nor less
than twenty, and be imprisoned not exceeding three months.

BE IT FURTHER ORDAINED, that if any Sailor or other person employed on board of any vessel now in this bay, or which may hereafter
come into it, run away and be caught within this town, such Sailor or other
person shall, on conviction of having run away, be ordered to hard labor
on the public works not exceeding six months.

BE IT FURTHER ORDAINED, that this Ordinance take effect from
and after the sixteenth day of September, A.D. 1847.

- - - -

AN ORDINANCE to amend an Ordinance passed on the 16th day of
September, 1847:

BE IT ORDAINED, that any person who shall apprehend any deserter
from any vessel within this harbor or bay, and produce evidence to convict
the person or persons of having run away from any vessel, shall be entitled
to a reward of fifty dollars for each person so convicted, to be paid by the
vessel from which they escaped, if they should again be taken on board,
and if not, out of the labor of such deserter on the public work of the town.

BE IT FURTHER ORDAINED, that the captains or owners of vessels

shall be allowed to deduct the said fifty dollars from the wages of the deserter.

BE IT FURTHER ORDAINED, that every deserter shall remain on
the public works, in addition to the time already provided in the ordinance
to which this is an amendment, until his labor at a fair price amounts to
the said reward, and all other expenses. . . .

POLICE REGULATIONS

BE IT ORDAINED BY THE TOWN COUNCIL OF THE TOWN OF SAN
FRANCISCO, that each and every member of the Council shall be a conser-
vator of the peace within the limits of the town, and shall issue any process
necessary to preserve the peace and morals of the place, upon application,
or when they may deem it proper so to do, and all such process shall be
made returnable to the Alcalde, and shall be charged and regarded by the
Alcalde as if it had been issued by himself.

BE IT FURTHER ORDAINED, that the members of the Council shall
receive no compensation for the performance of the above duty

BE IT ORDAINED BY THE TOWN COUNCIL OF THE TOWN OF SAN
FRANCISCO, that if any person shall enter the house occupied by another,
and assault the occupant or any other person within said house, such person so assaulting shall be fined, on proof thereof before the Alcalde, not
less than five nor more than fifty dollars; and on failure to pay the same,
shall be put upon the public works until the same is paid.

BE IT FURTHER ORDAINED, that any person who shall assault or
strike another in any other house than the one occupied by him, or in any
other place, such person so assaulting or striking shall be fined not less
than five nor more than fifty dollars; and on failure to pay, shall be put on
the public works until the same is paid.

BE IT FURTHER ORDAINED, that the informer shall have one half the
fine imposed by this ordinance.

BE IT FURTHER ORDAINED, that any person being guilty of improper
conduct in any house in this town, and being ordered to leave the same by
the occupant or persons employed by him, he shall, on failure to leave immediately after being so ordered, be taken before the Alcalde by any officer of the town, and fined not less than twenty, nor more than one hundred
dollars; and on failure to pay the fine,be put on the public works until the
fine is paid.

- - - -

Be it Ordained by the Council of the Town of San Francisco, that any
person firing a gun or pistol within one mile of Portsmouth Square, shall
be fined upon conviction thereof, not less than three nor more than five dollars.

Be it further Ordained, that any person killing or maiming the car-
rion fowls or birds within the limits of this town, shall be fined one dollar
for each offence, upon conviction thereof.

- - - -

Be it Ordained by the Council of the Town of San Francisco, that from

and after the 12th day of November, 1847, all property holders desiring to
dig wells upon their premises, or who may now have them dug, shall, under a penalty of fifty dollars fine, carefully close and fence, or box them
up.

- - - -

Resolved by the Town Council of the Town of San Francisco, that this
town shall not be held responsible for any expenses or charges for the keeping of any prisoner or prisoners confined in the calaboose or guard house,
for offences committed beyond the limits of the town, nor for the expenses
of State prisoners.

- - - -

Be it Ordained by the Town Council of San Francisco, that there shall
be sold, at public auction, a sufficient amount of the property of the Town
to meet all the appropriations made by the Council.

Be it further Ordained, that the sale shall commence on the 20th day
of December next, and that the same shall be advertised in the papers of
the town.

LICENSES

BE IT ORDAINED BY THE TOWN COUNCIL OF THE TOWN OF SAN
FRANCISCO, that any person or persons wishing to sell any merchandize
or property at auction, shall first procure a license from the constituted
authorities before selling, as hereby described.

BE IT ORDAINED, that the Alcalde of this town shall, on application
of any person or persons in writing, grant licenses to sell goods, wares
and merchandise, real estate and every other description of property, for
not less than one year; and for each of such licenses granted, the person
or persons shall pay the sum of twenty five dollars in advance.

BE IT FURTHER ORDAINED, that any person or persons acting in
the capacity of an Auctioneer without first obtaining licenses, shall be fined
not exceeding one hundred nor less than twenty five dollars, on conviction
thereof, with cost of suit.

BE IT FURTHER ORDAINED, that the Alcalde shall receive for his
fees one dollar for every such license so granted. The above to take effect
from and after the passage hereof, this 11th day of October, A.D. 1847.

- - - -

BE IT ORDAINED BY THE TOWN COUNCIL OF THE TOWN OF SAN
FRANCISCO, that from and after the passage hereof, no person or persons
shall sell or dispose of spiritous liquors in large or small quantities within the jurisdiction of this town, unless they have a license from the constituted authority. . . .

TOWN LOTS, IMPROVEMENTS, &c.

BE IT ORDAINED BY THE TOWN COUNCIL OF THE TOWN OF SAN
FRANCISCO, that the sum of one thousand dollars is hereby appropriated
for the erection of a pier at the foot of Broadway.

BE IT ORDAINED, that the pier shall be not less than ten feet wide,
and of sufficient heighth to resist the action of the sea and tide, and one

hundred and fifty feet in length, commencing at the rocks projecting from the bank, to be continued eastward in a parallel with Broadway.

BE IT FURTHER ORDAINED, that a committee of three be appointed to direct, superintend, and make contracts for the materials and work for the same, and report progress from time to time, when called on. Committee -- Messrs. Clark, Howard and Parker.

- - - -

At an adjourned meeting of Town Council, September 28, a law passed abrogating the conditions of building and fencing on grants of land within the limits of the town.

BE IT ORDAINED BY THE TOWN COUNCIL OF THE TOWN OF SAN FRANCISCO, that the acts of George Hyde, Esq., 1st Alcalde, granting more lots of land in this town and suburbs than one, to one person, are hereby ratified and confirmed.

- - - -

Be it Resolved by the Town Council of San Francisco, that all the unsold lots now belonging to the town of San Francisco, both on land and in the water, shall hereafter only be disposed of by public auction.

Special meeting of Council, October 28th, 1847.

- - - -

CONCERNING CONSTABLES

BE IT ORDAINED BY THE TOWN COUNCIL OF THE TOWN OF SAN FRANCISCO, that there shall be elected two Constables who shall constitute the chief police of the town.

BE IT FURTHER ORDAINED, that the Constables shall perform all duties required of other ministerial officers within the town; shall faithfully execute all process directed to them in accordance with law, and make due return thereof; shall strictly enforce and obey every law, ordinance and resolution, passed by the Council.

BE IT FURTHER ORDAINED, that the Constables shall receive for the service of any writ or other process, one dollar, to be paid out of the fines imposed upon cases; one dollar for the service of any writ or other process to be paid by the defeated party, also ten cents per mile for every mile which they may travel to serve any writ or other process beyond the limits of the town.

- - - -

AN ORDINANCE to amend an Ordinance concerning Constables.

Be it Ordained by the Town Council of San Francisco, that hereafter there shall be but one Constable for the Town, who shall receive, in addition to all the fees and perquisites of his office allowed by law, the sum of fifty dollars per month, and shall continue in office during good behaviour.

Be it further Ordained, that the Constable shall devote his entire time to his official duties, and is hereby empowered to arrest any one quity of any crime, misdemeanor, or other improper conduct, and take him or them before the Alcalde for trial.

Be it further Ordained, that the Constable shall have power to call upon any citizen or citizens to assist him in the performance of his duties, and that any person refusing to assist as aforesaid, shall be fined not less than five nor more than fifty dollars. . . .

THE GOLD RUSH, 1848

After the discovery of gold in California, hoards
of people descended on San Francisco, and over-
night built it into a metropolis, albeit composed
of canvas and packing boxes. It became a city
of tents and gambling houses, and a very cosmopolitan place. Bayard Taylor, who came by
steamer in 1849 as correspondent for a New York
paper, thus described the scene:

. . . We scrambled up through piles of luggage, and among the crowd col-
lected to witness our arrival, picked out two Mexicans to carry our trunks
to a hotel. The barren side of the hill before us was covered with tents
and canvas houses, and nearly in front a large two-story building displayed
the sign "Fremont Family Hotel."

As yet we were only in the suburbs of the town. Crossing the shoulder of the hill, the view extended around the curve of the bay, and hundreds
of tents and houses appeared, scattered all over the heights, and along the
shore for more than a mile. A furious wind was blowing down through a
gap in the hills, filling the streets with clouds of dust. On every side stood
buildings of all kinds, begun or half finished, and the greater part of them
mere canvas sheds, open in front, and covered with all kinds of signs, in
all languages. Great quantities of goods were piled up in the open air, for
want of a place to store them. The streets were full of people hurrying to
and fro, and of as diverse and bizarre a character as the houses; Yankees
of every possible variety, native Californians in serapes and sombreros,
Chilians, Sonorians, Kanakas from Hawaii, Chinese with long tails, Malays
armed with their everlasting creeses, and others in whose embrowned and
bearded visages it was impossible to recognize any especial nationality.
We came at last into the plaza, now dignified by the name of Portsmouth
Square. It lies on the slant side of the hill, and from a high pole in front
of a long one-story adobe building used as the Custom House, the American
flag was flying. On the lower side stood the Parker House, an ordinary
frame house of about sixty feet front -- and toward its entrace we directed
our course. . . .

FIRST CITY CHARTER OF SAN FRANCISCO, 1850

On April 15, 1850, the first city charter went into
effect. The Charter defined the geographic area
of the city, divided it into wards, and formed a
government composed of a Mayor and Council.

(Source: Manual of the Corporation of the City of San Francisco, San Francisco, 1852.)

Article I.
    1 The boundaries of the City of San Francisco shall be as follows:
the southern boundary shall be a line two miles distant, in a southerly direction, from the center of Portsmouth Square, and which line shall be parallel to the street known as Clay Street. The western boundary shall be a
line one mile and a half distant, in a westerly direction, from the center
of Portsmouth Square, and which line shall be parallel to the street known
as Kearney Street. The north and eastern boundaries shall be the same as
those of the county of San Francisco: but nothing in this section shall be
construed to divest or in any manner prejudice any right or priviledge to
which the city of San Francisco may be entitled beyond the limits above described.
    3 The city of San Francisco shall be divided into eight wards, which
shall not be altered, increased or diminished in number except by action of
the Legislater, so that each ward shall contain as near as may be, the
same number of white male inhabitants; the first council elected under this
charter shall divide the city into wards, and fix the bouneries thereof, in
accordance with this section.

Article II
    1 For the government of the city, there shall be elected a Mayor,
Recorder, and a Board of Aldermen, and a Board of Assistant Aldermen,
which two boards shall be styled the "Common Council," and each Board
shall consist of one member from each ward. There shall also be elected
by the city, a Treasurer, Comptroller, Street Commissioner, Collector of
City Taxes, City Marshal, City Attorney, and by each ward two Assessors.
No person shall be eligible to any of said offices, nor to any other office
which may be established by ordinance, nor shall any person be entitled to
vote for the same, who shall not be a qualified elector according to the Constitution and laws of the State, and who shall not have resided in the city
and in the ward or district for which he shall be elected or offer to vote,
for thirty days next preceding the election.
    5 At all elections for city offices, the voters shall vote by ballot, and
only in the wards where they respectively reside. . . .

8 No election shall be held in any grog-shop or other place where intoxicating liquor are vended.

Article III

Sect 1 The Mayor and Common Council shall have power within the city:

1 To make by-laws and ordinances not repugnant to the Constitution and laws of the United States or the State.

2 To levy and collect taxes not exceeding one per cent per annum upon all property made taxable by law for state purposes.

3 To borrow money and pledge faith of the city therefor, provided the aggregate amount of the debts of the city shall never exceed three times its annual estimated revenue.

4 To make regulations to prevent the introduction of contagious and other diseases into the city.

5 To establish hospitals, and to make regulations for the government of the same, and to secure the general health of the inhabitants.

6 To prevent and remove nuisances.

7 To erect water works either within or beyond the limits of the corporation, and provide the city with water.

8 To provide for licensing any and all business not prohibited by law.

9 To provide for the erection of all public buildings for the use of the city.

10 To establish, erect, and keep in repair, bridges, viaducts and all other useful improvements, and regulate the use of the same.

11 To license, tax, and regulate auctioneers, grocers, merchants, restaurants, and taverns, to be proportional to the amount of business done by each person, and to license, tax, regulate, and suppress ordenaries, hawkers, pedlers, brokers, pawnbrokers, and money changers.

13 To license and regulate porters, and fix the rate of porterage.

14 To license, tax, and regulate hackney carriages, wagons, carts, drays, and omnibusses, and fix the rates to be charged for the carriage of persons and the wagonage, cartage and drayage of property.

15 To license, tax, and regulate, and restrain bar-rooms, theatricals, and other exhibitions, shows and amusements.

16 To license, tax, restrain, prohibit, and suppress billiard tables, tippling houses, gaming and gambling houses, and to suppress baudy houses.

17 To erect market houses, establish markets and market places, and to provide for the government and regulation thereof.

18 To provide for the prevention of fires, and to organize and establish fire companies.

19 To regulate and prevent the carrying on of manufacturing of dangerous items in causing or producing fire; to appoint fire wardens and property guards and to compel any person or persons present to aid in extinguishing such fires and in preservation of property exposed to damage in time of fire, and by ordinance, to prescribe such other powers and duties as may be necessary on such occasions.

20 To regulate the weights, quality, and price of bread, to be sold within the city.

21 To provide for the appointment of all necessary officers, stewards, and agents of the corporation not otherwise provided for.

22 To establish and fix the salaries of the Mayor and all other officers, fix a tarriff of fare for the officer entitled to such, designate the fee which shall be allowed for each particular item of service, and cause the same to be published in like manner with the ordinance passed by the common Council.

23 To establish and regulate a police.

24 To impose fine, forfeiture and penalty, for the breaking of any ordinance.

25 To erect a workhouse or house of correction, and provide for the regulation and governance thereof.

26 To remove all obstructions from the side walks, and to provide for the construction, repair and cleaning of the same, and of the gutter.

27 To establish, support and regulate night watch and patrols.

28 To erect, repair, and regulate, public wharves, and docks; to regulate the erection and repair of private wharves, and fix the rates of wharfage thus erected.

29 To appropriate money for any item of city expenditure, and to provide for the payment of the debts and expenses of the city.

30 To operate, alter, abolish, widen, extend, establish, grade, pave, or otherwise improve, clean and keep in repair, streets and alleys; but no private property shall be taken without just compensation, as hereinafter provided for.

31 To regulate the storage of gunpowder, tar, pitch, resin and all other combustible materials, and the use of candles and lights in shops, stables, and other places; to prevent or remove any fire-place, stove, chimney, oven, boiler, or other apparatus, which may be dangerous in causing or promoting fires.

32 To regulate and prescribe the manner of building partition walls and fences.

33 To impose and appropriate fines, forfeitures, and penalties, for the breach of any ordinance, and to provide for the punishment of breakers of the city ordinances; but no fine shall be imposed of more than five hundred dollars, and no offender shall be imprisoned for a term longer than ten days.

34 To prevent and suppress any riot, rout, noise, disturbance, or disorderly assembly in any street, house, or place in the city. . . .

THE WOMAN PROBLEM, 1850

Like most frontier towns, San Francisco was
short of women. The following is an interesting commentary on that subject.

(Source: Russailh, Albert Bernard De, Last Adventure, San Francisco,
1931.)

When I first arrived here, there were only ten or twelve French women in San Francisco, but quite a number of American women had been
here for some time, and were living in attractive houses with a certain
amount of comfort and even luxury. They all had come from New York,
New Orleans, Washington, or Philadelphia and had the stiff carriage typical
of women in those cities. Men would look hopefully at them in the streets,
at least men who had just come to California, but they much preferred the
French women, who had the charm of novelty. Americans were irresistibly
attracted by their graceful walk, their supple but easy bearing, and charm-
ing freedom of manner, qualities, after all, only to be found in France; and
they trooped after a French woman whenever she put her nose out of doors,
as if they could never see enough of her. If the poor fellows had known
what these women had been in Paris, how one could pick them up on the bou-
levards and have them for almost nothing, they might not have been so free
with their offers of $500 or $600 a night. A little knowledge might have
cooled them down a bit. But I'm sure the women were flattered by so much
attention. Some of the first in the field made enough in a month to go home
to France and live on their income; but many were not so lucky, and one
still meets a few who have had a bad time and who are no better off finan-
cially than the day they stepped ashore. No doubt, they were blind to their
own wrinkles and faded skins, and were too confident of their ability to de-
ceive Americans regarding the dates on their birth-certificates.
Many ships have reached San Francisco during the past three or four
months, and the number of women in town has greatly increased, but a woman is still sought after and earns a lot of money. Nearly all the saloons
and gambling-houses employ French women. They lean on the bars, talk-
ing and laughing with the men, or sit at the card tables and attract players.
Some of them walk about with trays of cigars hanging in front of them;
others caterwaul for hours beside pianos, imagining they are singing like
Madame Stoltz. Occasionally, you will find one who hides her real business,
and pretends to be a dressmaker or a milliner; but most of them are quite
shameless, often scrawling their names and reception-hours in big letters
on their doors. There is a certain Madame Cassini who runs a collar shop
and claims to be able to predict the past, present, and future and anything
else you like.

To sit with you near the bar or at a card table, a girl charges one ounce ($16) an evening. She has to do nothing save honor the table with her presence. This hold true of the girls selling cigars, when they sit with you. Remember they only work in the gambling-halls in the evening. They have their days to themselves and can then receive all the clients who had no chance during the night. Of course, they often must buy new dresses, and dresses are very expensive out here.

For anything more you have to pay a fabulous amount. Nearly all these women at home were street-walkers of the cheapest sort. But out here, for only a few minutes, they ask a hundred times as much as they were used to getting in Paris. A whole night costs from $200 to $400.

You may find this incredible. Yet some women are quoted at even higher prices. I may add that the saloons and gambling-houses that keep women are always crowded and sure to succeed. . . .

THE FIRE OF MAY 4, 1851

One of the major problems of San Francisco
during this period was the recurrence of disastrous fires. The rapid population expansion
due to the gold rush created a town constructed
in large parts of wood and cloth. A slight acci-
dent in the heating or lighting system could start
a major fire. A second cause of the fires were
bands of thieves, feeding on the gold laden city,
and setting fire to it while they looted. The
problem was augmented by brisk prevailing
winds that blew in daily from the ocean, and a
shortage of proper fire fighting equipment which
did not increase in proportion to the town. Thus
the flames, once started, were almost impossible
to stop. The following description of the fire of
May 4, 1851 gives us a glimpse of the extent of
devastation, and some of the problems.

(Source: Hittell, John S., History of San Francisco, San Francisco, 1878.)

It really commenced a little before twelve on the night of the third of
May, but was called the fire of the fourth. It swept away the entire business portion of the city. . . . The burned distict was three quarters of a
mile long and a quarter of a mile wide, and more than fifteen hundred
houses were destroyed. Sixteen blocks were burned, including ten bounded
by Pine, Jackson, Kearney and Sansome; five bounded by Sansome, Battery,
Sacramento and Broadway; one bounded by Kearney, Montgomery, Washington and Jackson, and fractions of five other blocks. Many of the brick
buildings supposed to be fireproof, were unable to withstand the intense heat
of half a mile of flame fanned by a high wind. Vast quantities of goods
were destroyed. In some cases men stayed inside of the brick stores with
barrels of water, intending to risk their lives in the hope of saving their
buildings and goods. Twelve men were shut up in Neglee's building for
three hours in the midst of intense heat and almost suffocating smoke, but
they survived. Six who remained in the store of Taafe, McCahill & Co.
were not so fortunate.

THE SAN FRANCISCO FIRE DEPARTMENT OF 1851

The following newspaper editorial on the Fire Department gives us some idea of the inadequacy of that establishment.

(Source: The Evening Picayune, June 7, 1851.)

June 7, 1851: The Fire Department

The Report of the Chief Engineer, submitted to the Council last night, and which we publish in another place, represents the apparatus and houses of the Department to be in a most unfortunate state. Many of the engine houses were destroyed by the fire, many of the engines greatly damaged, the hose burned, and everything injured. The apparatus of the Hook and Ladder Companies are likewise in a generally damaged condition. The cisterns are, we believe, all either empty, or so much out of repair otherwise, as to render them useless. Mr. Kohler, Chief Engineer, asks that some action may be taken by the council in this emergency. Should a fire occur while the Department remains in its present crippled condition, nothing but the waters of the bay, and the naked sand-hills in the vicinity would check its course. The city treasury is hopelessly empty, and we see no prospect of immediate relief from that quarter. Our generous firemen have already expended their private means for the public good in organizing the Department, furnishing apparatus and keeping it in repair, to an extent that could not have been expected from them, and would never have been permitted any where but in San Francisco. Not a dollar has ever been refunded to them -- except in script -- and to expect them to make still further sacrifices, is unreasonable and unjust. What, then, shall be done? Must the Fire Department go to ruin, and the city to destruction, for the want of a few thousand dollars?

THE INCREASE AND IMPUNITY OF CRIME, 1851

> Uncontrollable crime was a problem as severe
> as uncontrollable fire. The police department,
> like the fire department proved inadequate for
> the job. The city, had grown faster than its in-
> stitutions, and the lure of gold attracted a crimi-
> nal element.

(Source: The Evening Picayune, January 6, 1851.)

The fact that scarce a day passes without the occurrence of one or
more bold and extensive robberies, and as frequent attempts upon life, is
creating a very general alarm and rendering the practice both necessary
and common for the citizens to carry arms for their defence. We are in-
clined to believe that there is an organized band of robbers, who have come
in upon us from the penal colonies of Great Britain, and who have, on system, established the means among themselves of shielding each other from
arrest, or from conviction and punishment, if arrested.

At all events, it is perfectly certain that the record of our criminal
courts, does not show that the detection and exposure of the depredations
upon our peace and property, bears anything like a just proportion to the
amount of crime detailed in the city items of our daily papers.

We know that the police corps are most particularly sensitive, to the
slightest imputation of fault to them of crimes committed; and we also know
that their force is not equal to the need we have to keep up an almost ubi-
quitous watch throughout the city. But for some cause, the fact stands out
before the knowledge of all men, that out of the immediate vicinity of the
gambling and drinking saloons, a policeman is scarce ever to be found, day
or night. For ourselves we must adopt the language which we hear from
almost every other man, that in the range of our walks we almost never
see a policeman. From Portsmouth Square to the head of Clay street, we
walk every night at all hours, early and late, and we have never seen at any
hour, or in any night, a policeman or watchman on that street, within those
limits. We hear the same thing said by gentlemen who are equally in the
necessity and habit of traversing at night, almost every other street leading from the centre of the city.

From the fact that the number in the police service is so small, that
their several whereabouts may be easily known to a concerted band of
rogues, renders it easy for them to pursue their depredations without exposure; and the other fact that when they are by chance discovered, and put
under arrest, and even when convicted of guilt, the punishment is either
evaded altogether, or is made so light by either the leniency of the law or
the magistrate, that it loses its terror in which lies the power of prevention

of crime will go on to still more appalling extremes, unless a more summary and severe treatment than has as yet been practiced shall be visited
upon each and all who are found guilty before the courts. . . .

THE COUNTY JAIL, 1851

When San Francisco was a small frontier community, the brig Euphemia adequately served
as a jail. As the crimes increased with the population, it was evident that a larger, stronger
structure was needed as the following article
observed.

(Source: Evening Picayune, San Francisco, June 6, 1851.)

The rapid progress towards the completion of the County jail observ-
able under the management of Col. Hayes, and his efficient assistants,
gives pleasing hope that the jolly times prisoners have heretofore had of
getting into prison, and getting out again, are nearly over. Under the lately
defunct dynasty, the county of San Francisco paid in the course of about
eleven months, ninety thousand dollars towards the construction of the jail,
and at the end of the time -- and of the money -- the foundation of the building was nearly completed! The Sheriff, Col. Hayes, assisted by Capt. Lam-
bert, with a subscription of $1,000, made up by the citizens, has, in the
space of seven days, done more towards the completion of the prison, than
was effected by the County since the commencement of the work. A sufficient number of cells are finished, to receive from seventy-five to one hundred prisoners, and when they get into them, they will stay there. With
such men at the head of our prison system, we may safely effect real as
well as promised reforms. Marshal Crozier has now a place of safety to
cage rascals in, and they will have to study Jack Sheppard and the Newgate
Calendar very carefully, if they expect to devise means of escape for the
future.

CONSTITUTION OF THE FIRST VIGILANCE COMMITTEE, 1851

> By June of 1851, the lawlessness had exceeded
> all civilized bounds and a group of citizens de-
> cided to do what the authorities could not. On
> June 9, 1851 James Neall, George Oakes and
> Sam Brannan formed a vigilance committee com-
> posed of two hundred people and wrote the fol-
> lowing constitution.

(Source: Daily Chronicle, June 10, 1851.)

Whereas it has become apparent to the citizens of San Francisco that
there is no security for life and property either under the regulations of
society as it as present exists or under the laws as now administered, --
therefore, the Citizens whose names are hereto attached do unite themselves into an association for the maintenance of the peace and good order
of Society and the preservation of the lives and property of the Citizens of
San Francisco.

THE EXECUTION OF JENKINS, JUNE 10, 1851

The first action of the newly formed committee
of vigilance was to execute a man named Jenkins.
The following is an eye witness account of the
first lynching in the town of San Francisco.

(Source: Coleman, William T., "San Francisco Vigilance Committee,"
The Century Magazine, N.Y., November, 1891.)

The want of a strong organization among those who wished to preserve
peace and enforce the laws was severely felt. Those who had the largest
interests at stake felt that unless there could be united action and control
there might be introduced a system of mob law, which would ultimately be
more dangerous than the existing state of affairs. It was for this reason
that, on the 10th day of June, 1851, an organization was effected, and about
two hundred names were enrolled. . . . The objects of the committee were
"to watch, pursue, and bring to justice the outlaws infesting the city,
through the regularly constituted courts, if possible, through more summary process, if necessary." Each member pledged his word of honor,
his life, and his fortune for the protection of his fellow-members, and for
purging the city of its bad characters. After arranging for a concert of
action, watch-words and a signal to call the members to the rendezvous,
which was three taps of a fire-bell, the committee adjourned for the evening.

Scarcely half an hour had passed before the bell was tapped. On reach-
ing headquarters I found a number of gentlemen, and soon after there was
brought in a very large, rough, vicious looking man called Jenkins, an ex-
convict from Sydney, who had been caught in the theft of a safe from a store.
He was well known as a desperate character who had frequently evaded justice. The committee was organized immediately into a court, and Jenkins
was tried for the offense within an hour. The evidence was overwhelming;
he was promptly convicted and sentenced to be hanged that night. Jenkins's
bearing throughout the trial was defiant and insulting, and he intimated that
his rescue by his friends might be expected at any moment. We were notified by our officers that already the roughest and worst characters throughout the city were mustering in force to resist the committee. At the same
time scores of our best citizens came forward and enrolled themselves as
members, while others pledged their support in anything we might do.

I strenuously reisted the proposition to execute Jenkins that night . . .
and proposed that he should be held till next morning and then hanged in
broad daylight as the sun rose. Only a few agreed with me; there was much
nervousness; the very circumstances of his crime having been committed
at the moment of our organization and in defiance of it, and the threatened

attack on us by abandoned criminals, all tended to impress the committee
with the necessity of prompt action. Seeing that he must be hanged, I
moved that the prisoner have the benefit of clergy. This was granted, but
when the minister was left with him, the hardened criminal heaped the vilest insults on his venerable head. This hastened his doom, and his career
was quickly closed.

The next morning the work of the Vigilance Committee was heralded
throughout the State, and hundreds of citizens came forward and tendered
their approval of our acts and asked to be enrolled in our ranks. The un-
expected arrest and quick execution of Jenkins spread consternation among
all his class. The Governor of the State, McDougal, issued a proclamation
and maintained a nominal opposition to the committee, but took no active
measures against it. . . .

THE VIGILANCE COMMITTEE OF 1853

William Gillis was a friend and partner of
Mark Twain whom he met in 1864. In his
memoirs, which are also valuable for their
insights about Mark Twain, he writes a description of San Francisco during the gold
rush period. He relates his impressions of
the Barbary Coast, the lawlessness, and the
assasination of James King of William, the
event that led to the formation of the vigilance committe of 1853.

(Source: Gillis, William, Gold Rush Days with Mark Twain, N.Y., 1930.)

In 1853 San Francisco was the most lawless city in the United States.
Criminals of every degree, from the "hold-up" man to the petty thief, gathered there. Nearly the whole of Happy Valley was populated by ex-con-
victs from Australia, known as the "Sydney Ducks." These men and women were of a type bestial, bodily and mentally, unclean. Their children
were leprous offspring of leprous parents. Growing up in an environment
of debauchery and crime, they became the notorious gang of thugs and
thieves known as the "Tar Flat Hoodlums," whose depredations were widespread over the territory south of Market Street, and were a terror to the
decent residents of that locality. Belated wayfarers were waylaid and
robbed, beaten into insensibility and left where they fell. Women and girls
were grossly insulted on the streets, and on two occasions when an officer
interfered he was assaulted and cruelly beaten. . . .

Another hotbed of iniquity was the "Barbary Coast." Here were nightly a
assembled the vilest gang of criminals the world over, men and women, de-
void of humanity and pity, robbing and killing for what they found on the
persons of their victims. Woe to the stranger with anything of value in his
possession who entered one of their dens alone! Trapped like a rat, he
would be robbed, murdered, and his body thrown into the bay. There was
seldom a week passed without a dead man being found floating in the bay,
while a crushed skull, knife wound, or a cord twisted around his neck plainly told the manner of his death. . . .

Gambling was run wide open throughout the city. Every game of chance
known in the world was played there, from faro down to craps. There were
more than a score of gambling hells in the city where the "hogging" game
of faro was played.

Principal among these was "El Dorado," located at Kearney Street between Washington and Clay. This place was packed day and night by men
of every vocation; working men, business men and men of leisure gathered

there by the hundreds, all trying to harvest a portion of the great wealth
displayed on the tables. There were twelve of these tables, every one of
them having its full quota of the votaries of Dame Chance.

Placer mining in California was then at its apex and the production of
gold from this source was enormous.

Thousands and thousands of dollars worth of this metal found its way to
San Francisco in its virgin state, brought there by miners who had washed
it from the earth. Some of these miners came to spend their money in having a "good time"; others were on their way to their families and sweet-
hearts in the East with the earnings of years of toil and privation in the
mines.

Most of the gold found its way into the coffers of those who ran these
games of faro. At each table the dealer had a pair of gold scales beside
him, and when a miner would place his bet on a card, the gold would be
weighed, and in case the miner won the dealer would pay, placing a valua-
tion of sixteen dollars per ounce on the gold, none of which was worth less
than eighteen dollars, some of it as much as twenty dollars, so, whether
the miner won or lost, the gambler got at least two dollars of his money.

All of these hells had men known as cappers, employed to keep a look-
out for these men from the mines, and upon their arrival, to lure them to
the games. Every boarding house, all the saloons and dance halls, in fact
every place of public resort in the city, had a representative from one of
these "tiger's dens." A capper would at once "spot" a miner among a
crowd in any of these places, and if he found that he was not with a friend
or party of friends, would approach and scrape an acquaintance with him,
sometimes in a friendly way, calling his attention to something taking place
in the crowd around them, then asking him to drink.

He would finally propose a walk to take in the sights, claiming that he,
too, was a stranger in the city, and did not care to make the rounds alone
at night, saying that it was not safe to do so. The miner, pleased to have
a friend with him, would at once consent. After an hour or so passed in
sight-seeing, the stroll would wind up at a faro game. Here the man from
the mountains would soon play in all his money. Broke, and filled with
booze, he would stagger into the street, where he would probably be arrested as a common drunk and pass the rest of the night in the city prison.

Prominent gambling houses were those of Steve Whipple on Sacramento
Street, between Kearney and Montgomery; Billy Burrows' on Montgomery,
norht of Bush; and that of Colonel Jack Gamble on Bush Street, between
Montgomery and Sansome. These games were ostensibly run on the square,
and were supposed to be patronized by gentlemen only. But these "square"
games always got away with the gentlemen's money, and were the cause of
several of them serving terms in the state's prison at San Quentin.

Gambling was bad enough, but it was not the heaviest burden under which
the people of San Francisco were groaning. Crime and gross immorality
held carnival. Men were held up and robbed in broad daylight on some of
the principal streets. Women of the underworld brazenly promenaded the

streets and openly solicited for the houses of ill fame. One of these women, the famous Rose Cooper, employed a brass band to give two concerts a week from the balcony of her mansion on Pike Street, when the "girls" would go into the assembled crowd and invite the "boys" to enter.

The water front was lined with low sailor boarding houses into which the sea-faring man was drawn. When his purse became empty -- the most of his money having gone into the till of his landlord -- he would be drugged and shipped to sea again, the landlord drawing most of his pay for the voyage, claiming the sailor was in debt to him for the amount drawn.

The theaters, with the exception of one or two, were pandering to the lowest instinct of the human race, two of them, the Lyceum and Bella Union, nightly staging plays of the vilest and most indecent character.

There were scores of places where the brutal sports of rat killing and dog and chicken fighting took place. For the conditions existing in San Francisco, the community had no remedy. The courts were powerless to punish law breakers who had sufficient means to put up a defense. The halls of justice swarmed with professional jurymen, and a rich criminal had no difficulty in securing as many of these on his jury as were needed to block a conviction.

All this culminated in the Assassination of James King of William by James P. Casey, an ex-convict from New York, who was then publishing a newspaper in the interests of the lawless class in San Francisco.

Mr. King had been exposing Casey's criminal life in the East in the Evening Bulletin. Casey went to the office of the Bulletin and demanded that King quit persecuting him, saying that if he did not stop publishing his scurrilous articles he (Casey) would kill him. Mr. King published the interview with Casey and kept right on exposing his past. Casey, exasperated by Mr. King's course, on the 14th of May, 1856, put his threat into execution by shooting him down in cold blood as he was walking along Montgomery Street near Washington.

When it was made known that Mr. King had been murdered by Casey, the people of San Francisco went wild with anger and grief. With forty-eight hours after the murder, at the call of "33 Secretary," more than five thousand of San Francisco's best citizens met and organized a "Committee of Vigilance." . . .

THE BRODERICK-TERRY DUEL AND THE SLAVERY ISSUE, SEPTEMBER, 1859

David Terry was a Southerner and a supporter of slavery. David Broderick was a Northerner and against the institution. The differences between the two men symbolized the split in pre Civil War California and the city of San Francisco. In 1859, a disputed election led to a duel and the death of Broderick. Popular sentiment went against Terry and was one of the factors that held California for the Union.

(Source: Hittell, Theodore H., _History of California_, San Francisco, 1885.)

At the appointed time the parties and their friends . . . examined the ground. There were about eight other persons present. Each principal was accompanied by his seconds and a group of friends.

A few matters, including the important one as to choice of weapons, had been left for determination on the ground; and they were now settled by tossing up a half dollar. Terry won the choice of weapons. . . . Broderick won the choice of ground and the giving of the word. The pistols were examined and the one intended for Broderick loaded by the armorer, and that intended for Terry by his friend, Samuel H. Brooks, while the principals were placed in position fronting each other. It was a raw cold morning; both wore overcoats, which they now threw off, and appeared in full, black suits, their frock coats buttoned across the breast, and without shirt collars. Each had given over to one of his seconds the contents of his pockets and each was then what was called examined, to see that he wore no armor, by a second of his adversary, and handed his pistol. Each stood erect; Broderick with his black, soft-wool hat drawn down over his eyes, while Terry had his hat of similar kind thrown over his forehead; and each though firm and rigid, showed evident signs of repressed excitement -- Terry, however, being much cooler than Broderick. The word, as it was to be given by Colton (Broderick's second) was then plainly stated, or what in dueling phrase is called exemplified, by him and repeated by Benham. (Terry's second.) The seconds stepped back and the principals stood alone, each with his cocked pistol pointing down at his side.

By this time it was nearly seven o'clock. Colton in a clear voice asked, "Gentlemen, are you ready?" Terry replied at once, "Ready," but Broderick hesitated a moment, adjusting his weapon, and then answered, with a nod to Colton, "Ready." Then came the word, "Fire -- one-- two." At the word "one," as Broderick was raising his pistol, it went off and the ball struck the ground nine or ten feet from him but in direct line with his antagonist. Before the word "two," Terry fired. There was a slight show of dust upon the right lapel of Broderick's buttoned coat, indicating where Terry's ball had struck. In a moment Broderick involuntarility raised his arms; there was a visible shuddering of the body and then a contraction of the right hand, from which the pistol ahd dropped to the ground. A violent convulsion of his frame next took place; there was a turn toward the left; his body sank; his left knee gave way, then his right, and he fell half prostrate, his left arm supporting him from falling flat. His seconds and surgeons rushed to his aid. . . .

Terry . . . deliberately folded his arms and stood perfectly still.

Broderick died three days later. His friends said that he was deliberately murdered. They pointed out that the pistols had been supplied by Terry and that the one given to Broderick had a defect in it. This had caused it to discharge prematurely thus giving Terry and excuse for firing before the signal.

At all events, Terry was looked upon by many as "a man with the mark of Cain upon his brow," whereas Broderick became great in his martyrdom. His death made him the symbol of a cause. Without doubt it did much to crystallize public sentiment in California against slavery.

The homage paid Broderick at his death was only equal to the homage paid the memory of James King of William, his enemy, a few years before. The State legislature even appropriated money to put a monument over his grave.

As a child, passing this broken shaft in Laurel Hill cemetery, I used to feel a spasm of fear at what its shattered top implied -- a life snuffed out by violence.

THE FIRST TRANSCONTINENTAL RAILROAD, 1869

> As gold had built the city in one era, the railroad
> was to build it in the next. The following editorial
> in the Evening Bulletin reflected the anticipation
> that the transcontinental railroad would stimulate
> the further growth of the city.

(Source: The Evening Bulletin, May 8, 1869.)

We can now leave San Francisco in the morning by the steamer New
World and be landed in an hour and a quarter at Vallejo, from which place
we shall be carried by rail to New York or whatever point we may desire
to reach in the Atlantic States. Possibly within the next week the road will
be in such order as to take passengers from San Francisco to New York in
one week, and within a month we may anticipate making the trip in about
six days from ocean to ocean. If we be not disappointed in our anticipations
. . . a person will be able to leave San Francisco and be in London or Paris
in from fifteen to seventeen days. . . .

It would be folly to say that quick communication will not stimulate trade.
Changes must take place in the affairs of this coast, and we are on the con-
fines of a large population, being no longer isolated from the rest of the
Union. The Mississippi Valley is but four or five days from us, with its
teeming millions. It is in fact not much more difficult for the inhabitants
of Illinois, Missouri, Iowa, Indiana, etc., to reach us than it is for them
to reach New York. . . . Railroads changed the condition of the Mississippi
Valley and made it comparatively an empire. Railroads are now about to
change the aspect of things in California. What this will be and how rapidly
it will come around, no man can precisely determine, but of one thing we
may rest assured: we are no longer an isolated community.

THE BARBARY COAST, 1875

San Francisco was born as a shipping port, grew
with the gold rush, and continued to expand as a
transportation center. The city was cosmopolitan,
the West was wild, and the laws were lax; hence,
a section developed known as the Barbary Coast,
which made San Francisco a typical "sailor's" town.
As the city matured, moralists started to attach
this section and finally succeeded in eliminating
most vice from it. The following article is an example of this moralistic crusade. Once past the
moralism, the reader receives an interesting picture of this colorful section, a section that helped
make San Francisco the vibrant, alive city that it
still is.

(Source: Lloyd, B.E., Lights and Shades in San Francisco, San Francisco,
1876.)

"Barbary Coast" proper is in the northerly part of the city, comprising
both sides of Broadway and Pacific streets, and the cross streets between'
them, from Stockton street to the water front. Nearly the whole length of
Dupont street, running south from Broadway, and many of its interesting
by-ways might be called the highlands to this region, as most of the dwel-
lers therein are perhaps not a whit less immoral and vicious; and only for
the distinction that rich apparel and some of the refining accomplishments
bestow, would be classed in the same social grade. Like the malaria arising from a stagnant swamp and poisoning the air for miles around, does
this stagnant pool of human immorality and crime spread its contaminating
vapors over the surrounding blocks on either side. Nay, it does not stop
here, for even the remotest parts of the city do not entirely escape its pol-
luting influence.

It is true that inside the limits of Barbary Coast, even among its foulest
dens, are some who witness from day to day the lowest phases of human de-
pravity and yet remain undefiled. These are not there by choice; but by
force of circumstances are compelled to abide in the unhallowed precincts.
But the great number of those who dwell there have chosen the locality as
the most fitting place wherein to pursue their respective callings.

In the early days of San Francisco, Barbary Coast was the place of refuge
and security for the hundreds of criminals that infested the city. When they
had passed within its boundary, they were strongly fortified against any assault that the officers of the law might lead against them. It was, in those
days, an easy matter for a stranger to enter this fortress of vice, but when

once behind the walls he was exceedingly fortunate who had the opportunity
to depart, taking with him his life. Then villains of every nationality held
high carnival there. The jabber of the Orient, the soft-flowing tone of the
South Sea Islander, the guttural gabbings of the Dutch, the Gallic accent,
the round full tone of the son of Africa, the melodious voice of the Mexicano,
and the harsh, sharp utterances of the Yankee, all mingled in the boisterous
revels.

It was a grand theatre of crime. The glittering stiletto, the long bowie
knife, the bottle containing the deadly drug, and the audacious navy revolver, were much-used implements in the plays that were there enacted.
There was no need to mimic dying groans, and crimson water, for the drawing of warm heart-blood and the ringing of real agonizing moans of death
only, would be recognized as the true style of enacting tragedy.

Were the restraining powers of the law and public sentiment removed,
Barbary Coast to-day could soon develop the same kind of outlawry that
made it notorious in the primitive days. The material is ready at all times,
and should the favorable circumstances transpire to kindle it into destructive activity, scenes as startling as those that won for the locality it chris-
tening, would be reenacted. Even in the presence of a strong police force,
and in the face of frowning cells and dungeons, it is unsafe to ramble
through many of the streets and lanes in this quarter. Almost nightly there
are drunken carousels and broils, frequently terminating in dangerous violence; men are often garroted and robbed, and it is not by any means a rare
occurrence for foul murder to be committed. "Murderers Corner" and
"Deadman's Alley" have been rebaptized with blood over and over again,
and yet call for other sacrifices.

Barbary Coast is the haunt of the low and vile of every kind. The petty
thief, the house burglar, the tramp, the whoremonger, lewd women, cut-
throats and murderers, all are found there. Dance houses and concert
saloons, where blear-eyed men and faded women drink vile liquor, smoke
offensive tobacco, engage in vulgar conduct, sing obscene songs, and say
and do everything to heap upon themselves more degradation, unrest and
misery, are numerous. Low gambling houses thronged with riot-loving
rowdies in all stages of intoxication are there. Opium dens, where heathen
Chinese and God forsaken women and men are sprawled in miscellaneous
confusion, disgustingly drowsy, or completely overcome by inhaling the
vapors of the nauseous narcotic, are there. Licentiousness, debauchery,
pollution, loathsome disease, insanity from dissipation, misery, poverty,
wealth, profanity, blasphemy and death, are there. And Hell, yawning to
receive the putrid mass, is there also.

THE CHINESE PROBLEM, 1879

San Franciscans were never too friendly towards
the Chinese, but would tolerate them when times
were good. Unfortunately, when times were bad
the Chinese, who would work for less money than
the native Americans, were blamed. In addition,
Chinese immigration did not cease when the railroads were completed. The contracting companies
and the steamship companies still recruited and
imported them, deeming their passage necessary
to the lines' financial survival.

(Source: The San Francisco Chronicle, March 6, 1879.)

Coolies are such pauper Chinese as are hired in bulk and by contract at
Chinese ports, to be hired out by the contracting party in this or any other
foreign country to which by the terms of the contract, they are shipped.
The contracting parties for California are the Six Companies, and they
have imported more than nine-tenths of all the Chinese who have come to
this State . . . When the Coolie arrives here, he is as rigidly under the
control of the contractor who brought him, as ever an African Slave was
under his master in South Carolina or Louisiana. There is no escape from
the contractor or the contract. . . .

THE PALACE HOTEL, 1875

In the 70's, San Francisco was made wealthy by the
discovery of silver in Nevada, the famous Comstock
Lode. This stroke of fortune, like the past ones,
caused a new boom period. It also created a new
crop of millionaires who wanted to display their
wealth. In the building boom that occurred, opu-
lent structures were erected such as William C.
Ralston's Palace Hotel, which was the grandest
in the world. It is interesting to note, in the following description of the hotel, the writer's fears
of earthquakes, which were ungrounded. The Hotel
survived so well that at a later date, $90,000 had
to be spent to tear it down.

(Source: Springfield Daily Republican, August 31, 1875.)

The great feature now in the building line, in the city, is the erection of
the nearly completed Palace Hotel, and it is really a mammoth building and
enterprise. It occupies an entire block, covering an area of over ninety-
six thousand square feet, and is bounded by Market, New Montgomery,
Jessie and Annie streets. It is eight stories high, and from all parts of the
city, or its approaches, this immense pile of brick and iron towers up
above everything else. There are over seven hundred rooms, and it contains three miles of hall and thirty miles of steam and gas pipe. Nearly
twenty-five millions of brick and three thousand tons of iron were consumed
in its construction, and thirteen hundred men have been at work upon the
building at one time.

I walked into the superintendent's office, and although the work now is
all done "but finishing" I found nine hundred and fifteen men at work, of
whom three hundred and fifty-six were carpenters, two hundred and eighty-
five were painters, twenty-one plumbers, thirty-four gas fitters, and so on
through all the departments. Fifty thousand yards or twenty-eight miles
of carpet are now being laid and the contract for the silver-ware, which is
being made by Gorham at Providence, is rising of sixty thousand dollars.

There are over one thousand windows, three hundred and sixty bay windows, and if the building is ever lighted at one time, with eight thousand
gas burners, it must be well worth seeing. There are three courts, the
center one having an iron-framed glass covering, with a driveway, sidewalk and miniature park beneath it. There are vast artesian wells, five
elevators, and seven grand staircases, fire escapes, fire alarm telegraphs,
and a pneumatic despatch tube for carrying of messages and parcels to any
point on the different floors.

The hotel is calculated to accommodate twelve hundred guests, and the entire cost of the building and furnishing will not fall far short of five million dollars. . . .

A POEM FOR SAN FRANCISCO, 1870s

San Francisco has been and continues to be
the subject of poems, songs and stories. Bret
Harte, a famous author of stories about the
American West, composed the following short
ode to the city by the bay.

(Source: Bret Harte, San Francisco, New York, 1878.)

Serene, indifferent of Fate,
Thou sittest at the Western gate;
Thou seest the white seas strike the tents,
O warder of two continents
Thos drawest all things, small or great,
To Thee, beside the Western gate.

THE CABLE CARS OF SAN FRANCISCO, 1889

In 1889 Rudyard Kipling visited San Francisco
and described how the cable cars solved the
problems of hills in the city.

(Source: Kipling, Rudyard, <u>Letters from San Francisco</u>, San Francisco,
1949.)

   Later I began a vast but unsystematic exploration of the streets. I
asked for no names. It was enough that the pavements were full of white
men and women, the streets clanging with traffic, and that the restful roar
of a great city rang in my ears. The cable-cars glided to all points of the
compass. I took them one by one until I could go no farther. San Francisco has been pitched down on the sand-bunkers of the Bikaner desert. About
one-fourth of it is ground reclaimed from the sea -- any old-timer will tell
you all about that. The remainder is ragged, unthrifty sand-hills, pegged
down by houses.
   From an English point of view there has not been the least attempt at
grading those hills, and indeed you might as well try to grade the hillocks
of Sind. The cable-cars have for all practical purposes made San Francisco a dead level. They take no count of rise or fall, but slide equably on
their appointed courses from one end to the other of a six-mile street.
They turn corners almost at right angles; cross other lines, and, for all
I know, may run up the sides of houses. There is no visible agency of
their flight; but once in a while you shall pass a five-storied building, hum-
ming with machinery that winds up an everlasting wire cable, and the initi-
ated will tell you that here is the mechanism. I gave up asking questions.
If it pleases Providence to make a car run up and down a slit in the ground
for many miles, and if for two pence-half penny I can ride in that car, why
shall I seek the reasons of the miracle?

ANTI-CHINESE PREJUDICE, 1897

The following little glimpse of Chinatown
expresses the attitudes which led to the
anti-Chinese prejudice of the period.

(Source: The New York Times, November 29, 1897.)

We also went through Chinatown by daylight. You can do this on your
own hook and need no guide. We found everything as lively as a bee-hive,
and it was curious and interesting to go into their shops and watch how they
transact business. They know what their wares cost them, and just how
much they want for them, and you cannot buy them for any less. They are
as shrewd and sharp as any men I ever dealt with. Their stores are
small, but contain goods of rare qualities and great value. They are quick
at figures, and each of them have a figure-band with which they count with
a rapidity and precision that is wonderful. Dupont Street is lined with Chinese stores on both sides for five or six squares. You meet with such
names as Man, Hob & Co., Long Sing Young, Chee Kee, Ty Wing & Co.,
Si Potal, Chong We, Shun Yuen Hing & Co., Ah Ho, Che King Quong, Kum
Lung & Co., and Sun Ham Wah & Co., -- all these names imply something
that none but Chinamen can understand. Each establishment has its own
sign, and each sign is blessed. Yesterday was the birthday of the Emperor
of China. I went through Cinatown this afternoon. Every house-top was
mounted with a Chinese flag, many of them large and beautiful and made of
silk. All of them had large Chinese lanterns strung along in front of their
houses, and to-night the town was in a blaze of celestial glory. They wanted
to fire off crackers, but the Mayor would not allow it, and John is afraid to
do anything unless it is permitted. I asked one of them who can speak English very well, if he intended to explode some fireworks to-night. His reply was, "Melican man no lettee. Chinaman no goodee." The feeling
against the Chinese is intense, but not from all classes. The laboring man
and the mechanic are his bitter foes, and really we cannot blame them.
After seeing how the Chinese live and the small wages they make and the
kind of food they eat and the low dens, or rather holes, they live in, I trust
in God that American labor and working men shall never be placed on a level with it. The only way to stop it is to stop it; just as the only way to resume specie payment was to resume.

CHINATOWN, 1900

During the construction of the transcontinental
railroad, numerous Chinese were imported to
serve as a cheap source of labor on the construction gangs. Many migrated to San Francisco, where they formed the largest Chinese
community in the United States. Their different customs and manners have always fasci-
nated travelers and much has been written about
them. The following is a description of Chinatown and the Chinese in 1900.

(Source: Keeler, Charles, San Francisco and Thereabout, San Francisco,
1902.)

A few blocks up Kearny Street from the corner of Market is a stretch of
green popularly known as the Plaza, but officially designated Portsmouth
Square. . . The spot is teeming with memories of the early days. Here
the American flag was first raised by Captain Montgomery of the Sloop-of-
war Portsmouth. Here the Vigilance Committee first took the law into its
own hands. The Parker House, and afterward the Jenny Lind Theatre,
stood on the site now occupied by the Hall of Justice, a fine new building
with a clock tower, situated on Kearny Street just opposite the Plaza. In
the days of '49 the town life centered about this square, and many public
meetings of importance were held here during those intensely dramatic
days.

Today Portsmouth Square is the lungs of Chinatown--the one breathing
space in that strange Oriental city which crowds down upon the greenery of
the little park. . . .

Here is a gragment of one of the oldest and most conservative civiliza-
tions, grafted upon the newest and most radical. Certain innovations of
up-to-date Americanism the Chinese have adopted. They have a telephone
central station with native operators, and many of their buildings are illum-
inated with incandescent lamps, but these things are external and superfi-
cial. Two thousand years of arrested development is not conducive to a
pliable mind. The Chinaman who uses the telephone, eats with chopsticks
and goes before his joss with presents of food to propitiate the god and make
his business prosper. His queue is as sacred to him as it was to his fore-
fathers. He will run a sewing machine and drive a broken down plug hitched
to a dilapidated laundry wagon, but when it comes to delivering vegetables
he swings two immense baskets from a pole across his shoulder, and runs
mechanically along with a weight that would appall a white man. . . .

The buildings of Chinatown are abandoned stores and dwellings of the

white population, more or less made over by the addition of balconies and
such other changes as the requirement or fancies of their present owners
may suggest. The restaurants and joss houses are particularly striking
on account of their deep balconies, ornamented with carved woodwork
brightly colored or gilded, and set off with immense lanterns and with big
plants in china pots. About whatever these strange people do there is an
elusive, indefinable touch, which is distinctively racial and picturesque. . . .

THE CITY CHARTER OF 1900

This city charter was proposed in 1897, ratified
on May 26, 1898, and put in force January 8, 1900.
It was designed to bring good government to the
city by virtue of public meetings of the Board of
Supervisors. However, it had the opposite effect.
The mayor had broad power to appoint judges and
police commissioners and there was also little way
·to fix responsibility. Therefore, Mayor Schmitz
and Abe Ruef were able to use this charter to control the city and initiate a period of municipal corruption almost unparalleled in the city's history.

THE BOARD OF SUPERVISORS.

Legislative Power.

Section 1. The legislative power of the City and County of San Francisco
shall be vested in a legislative body, which shall be designated the Board of
Supervisors. Such body is also designated in this Charter, the Supervisors.

Supervisors: Term. Qualfications.

Sec. 2. The Board of Supervisors shall consist of eighteen members,
all of whom shall hold office for two years and be elected from the City and
County at large. Each one must be at the time of his election an elector of
the City and County, and must have been such for at least five years next
preceding his election. Each Supervisor shall receive a salary of two hundred dollars a month.

Every person who has served as Mayor of the City and County, so long
as he remains a resident thereof, shall be entitled to a seat in the Board of
Supervisors and to participate in its debates, but shall not be entitled to a
vote nor to any compensation. -- As amended November 15, 1910; approved
by the Legislature February 17, 1911 (Statutes, 1911, page 1661).

Quorum

Sec. 3. A majority of all the members of the Board shall constitute a
quorum, but a less number may adjourn from day to day and compel the at-
tendance of absent members in such manner and under such penalties as the
Board may prescribe.

Powers of the Board of Supervisors.

Sec. 4. The Board shall:

Appointments.

1. Appoint a Clerk, Sergeant-at-Arms and, when authorized to do so by ordinance, such additional clerks and other assistants as may be deemed necessary.

Rules.

2. Establish rules for its proceedings.

Journal.

3. Keep a journal of its proceedings, and allow the same to be published. The ayes and noes shall on demand of any member be taken and entered therein.

4. Have authority to punish its members for disorderly or contemptuous behavior in its presence.

Presiding Officer.

Sec. 5. The Mayor shall be the presiding officer of the Board of Supervisors. In the absence of the Mayor the Board shall appoint a presiding officer pro tempore from its own members, who shall have the same right to vote as other members.

Meetings: Time and Place.

Sec. 6. The Board shall meet on Monday of each week, or if that day be a legal holiday, then on the next day. The Board shall not adjourn to any other place than to its regular place of meeting, except in case of great necessity or emergency. The meetings of the Board shall be public.

Clerk of the Board: Duties and Powers.

Sec. 7. The Clerk of the Board, when requested to do so, shall administer oaths and affirmations, without charge, in all matters pertaining to the affairs of his office, and shall perform such services as may be prescribed by the Board. He shall have the custody of the seal, and of all leases, grants and other documents, records and papers of the City and County. His signature shall be necessary to all leases, grants and conveyances for the City and County.

Ordinances: Enactment and Passage.

Sec. 8. Every legislative act of the City and County shall be by ordinance. The enacting clause of every ordinance shall be in these words: "Be it ordained by the People of the City and County of San Francisco as follows." No ordinance shall be passed except by bill, and no bill shall be so amended as to change its original purpose.

Bills and Resolutions: Final Adoption.

Sec. 9. No bill shall become an ordinance, nor resolution be adopted, unless finally passed by a majority of all the members of the Board and the vote be taken by ayes and noes and the names of the members voting for and against the same be entered in the Journal.

Revision and Amendment.

Sec. 10. No ordinance shall be revised, re-enacted or amended by reference to its title; but the ordinance to be revised or re-enacted, or the section thereof amended, shall be re-enacted at length as revised and amended.

Subject and Title.

Sec. 11. An ordinance shall embrace but one subject, which subject shall be expressed in its title. If any subject be embraced in an ordinance and not expressed in its title, such ordinance shall be void only as to so much thereof as is not expressed in its title.

Reconsideration: Franchises.

Sec. 12. When a bill is put upon its final passage in the Board and fails to pass, and a motion is made to reconsider, the vote upon such motion shall not be acted upon before the expiration of twenty-four hours after adjournment. No bill for the grant of any franchise shall be put upon its final passage within ninety days after its introduction, and no franchise shall be renewed before one year prior to its expiration. Every ordinance shall, after amendment, be laid over for one week before its final passage.

Advertisement of Bills and Resolutions.

Sec. 13. Every bill or resolution providing for any specific improvement, or the granting of any franchise or privilege, or involving the lease, appropriation or disposition of public property, or the expenditure of public money, except sums less than two hundred dollars, or levying any tax or assessment, and every ordinance providing for the imposition of a new duty or penalty, shall, after its introduction, be published in the official newspaper with the ayes and noes, for at least five successive days (Sundays and legal holidays excepted) before the final action upon the same. If such bill be amended, the bill as amended shall be advertised for a like period before the final action thereon. But in cases of great necessity the officers and heads of departments may, with the consent of the Mayor, expend such sums of money, not to exceed two hundred dollars, as shall be necessary to meet the requirements of such necessity.

Veto of Separate Items by the Mayor.

Sec. 14. If any bill be presented to the Mayor containing several items appropriating money or fixing a tax levy, he may object to one or more items separately, while approving other portions of the bill. In such case he shall append to the bill at the time of signing it a statement of the item or items to which he objects and the reasons therefor, and the item or items so objected to shall not take effect unless passed notwithstanding the Mayor's objection. Each item so objected to shall be separately reconsidered by the Board in the same manner as bills which have been disapproved by the Mayor.

When Ordinances Take Effect.

Sec. 15. No ordinance shall take effect until ten days after its passage unless otherwise provided in such ordinance.

Approval or Disapproval of Mayor.

Sec. 16. Every bill and every resolution as hereinbefore provided, which shall have passed the Board and shall have been duly authenticated, shall be presented to the Mayor for his approval. The Mayor shall return such bill or resolution to the Board within ten days after receiving it. If he approves it he shall sign it and it shall then become an ordinance. If he disapproves it he shall specify his objections thereto in writing. If he does not return it with such disapproval within the time above specified, it shall take effect as if he had approved it. The objections of the Mayor shall be entered at large in the Journal of the Board, and the Board shall, after five and within thirty days after such bill or resolution shall have been so returned, reconsider and vote upon the same. If the same shall, upon reconsideration, be again passed by the affirmative vote of not less than fourteen members of the Board, the presiding officer shall certify that fact on the bill or resolution, and when so certified, the bill shall become an ordinance with like effect as if it had been approved by the Mayor. If the bill or resolution shall fail to receive the vote of fourteen members of the Board it shall be deemed finally lost. The vote on such reconsideration shall be taken by ayes and noes and the names of the members voting for and against the same shall be entered in the Journal. . . .

Deposit of All Ordinances.

Sec. 17. All ordinances and resolutions shall be deposited with the Clerk of the Board, who shall record the same at length in a suitable book.

Repeal of Ordinances.

Sec. 18. No ordinance shall be repealed except by ordinance adopted in the manner hereinbefore set out, and such ordinance shall be presented to the Mayor for his approval as hereintofore provided.

Demands for Payment of Money.

Sec. 19. Except as provided in Chapter III of Article III of this Charter, all demands payable out of the treasury must, before they can be approved by the Auditor or paid by the Treasurer, be first approved by the Board of Supervisors. All demands for more than two hundred dollars shall be presented to the Mayor for his approval, in the manner hereinbefore provided for the passage of bills or resolutions. All resolutions directing the payment of moeny other than salaries or wages, when the amount exceeds five hundred dollars, shall be published for five successive days (Sundays and legal holidays excepted) in the official newspaper.

Sec. 20. Repealed by amendment November 15, 1910; approved by the Legislature February 17, 1911 (Statutes, 1911, page 1661).

Sec. 21. Repealed by amendment November 15, 1910; approved by the Legislature February 17, 1911 (Statues, 1911, page 1661).

Amendments to Charter by Petition.

Sec. 22. Whenver there shall be presented to the Supervisors a petition signed by a number of voters equal to fifteen per centum of the votes cast at the last preceding State of municipal election, asking that an amendment or amendments to this Charter, to be set out in such petition, be submitted to the people, the Board must submit to the vote of the electors of the City and County the proposed amendment or amendments.

The signatures to the petition need not all be appended to one paper. Each signer shall add to his signature his place of residence, giving the street and number. One of the signers of each such paper shall make oath before an officer competent to administer oaths that the statements made therein are true and that each signature to such paper appended is the genuine signature of the person whose name purports to be thereto subscribed.

The Board of Election Commissioners must make all necessary provision for submitting the proposed amendment or amendments to the electors at a special election to be called by it, and shall canvass the vote in the same manner as in other cases of election.

All the provisions of the Constitution of the State embracing the subject in this section provided for are hereby expressly made applicable to such proposed amendment or amendments. But if at any time there shall be no constitutional provision or provisions under which this Charter may be amended, then the aforesaid amendment or amendments must be submitted by the Board of Election Commissioners to the vote of the electors of the City and County at the election which next ensues after such petition is filed with the Supervisors, if any such election is not to be held within sixty days after the filing of such petition.

The tickets used at such election shall contain the words "FOR THE AMENDMENT" (stating the nature of the proposed amendment) and "AGAINST THE AMENDMENT" (stating the nature of the proposed amendment).

If a majority of the votes cast upon such amendment or amendments shall be in favor of the adoption thereof, the Board of Election Commissioners shall, within thirty days from the time of such election, proclaim such fact, and thereupon this Charter shall be amended accordingly.

PAYMENT OF CLAIMS.

Monthly Payment of Salaries.   Limitation Upon Demands.   Revival of Claims.

Section 1. The salaries and compensation of all officers, including policemen and employees of all classes, and all teachers in the public schools, and others employed at fixed wages, shall be payable monthly. Any demade upon the treasury accruing under this Charter shall not be paid, but shall be forever barred by limitation of time, unless the same be presented for payment, properly audited, within one month after such demand became due and payable; or, if it be a demand which must be passed and approved by the Supervisors or Board of Education, or by any other Board, then within one month after the first regular meeting of the proper Board held next after the demand accrued; or, unless the Supervisors shall, within six months after the demand accrued as aforesaid, on a careful examination of the facts, resolve that the same is in all respects just and legal, and the presentation of it, as above required, was not in the power either of the original party interested or his agent, or the present holder, in which case they may by ordinance revive such claim; but it shall be barred in the same manner unless presented for payment within twenty days thereafter. No valid demand arising subsequent to the claim which may be revived as aforesaid

shall be rendered invalid by reason of such revival exhausting the fund out
of which subsequent claims might otherwise be paid. Such revived claim
shall take rank as of the day of its revival.

THE MAYOR.

Qualifications. Term. Salary, Appointees in His Office. Salaries.

Section 1. The chief executive officer of the City and County shall be
designated the Mayor. He shall be an elector of the City and County at the
time of his election, and must have been such for at least five years next
preceding such time. He shall be elected by the people and hold office for
two years. He shall receive an annual salary of six thousand dollars. He
may appoint a Secretary, who shall receive an annual salary of twenty-four
hundred dollars; an usher, who shall receive an annual salary of nine hundred dollars; and a stenographer and typewriter, who shall receive an annual salary of nine hundred dollars. All of said appointees shall hold their
positions at the pleasure of the Mayor.

Mayor's Duties.

Sec. 2. The Mayor shall vigilantly observe the offical conduct of all
public officers and the manner in which they execute their duties and fulfill
their obligations. The books, records and official papers of all departments,
officers and persons in the employ of the City and County shall at all times
be open to his inspection and examination. He shall take special care that
the books and records of all departments, boards, officers and persons are
kept in legal and proper form. When any official defalcation or wilful neglect of duty or official misconduct shall come to his knowledge, he shall
suspend the delinquent officer or person from office pending an official investigation.

The Mayor shall from time to time recommend to the proper officers of
the different departments such measures as he may deem beneficial to public interest. He shall see that the laws of the State and ordinances of the
City and County are observed and enforced. He shall have a general super-
vision over all the departments and public institutions of the City and County, and see that they are honestly, economically and lawfully conducted,
and shall have the right to attend the meetings of any of the Boards provided
for in this Charter, and offer suggestions at such meetings. He shall take
all proper measures for the preservation of public order and the suppres-
sion of all riots and tumults, for which purpose he may use and command
the police force. If such police force is insufficient, he shall call upon the
Governor for military aid in the manner provided by law, so that such riots
or tumults may be promptly and effectually suppressed.

Execution of Public Contracts and Agreements. Actions to Annul Forfeited
Franchises. Postpone Franchises.

Sec. 3. The Mayor shall see that all contracts and agreements with the
City and County are faithfully kept and fully performed. It shall be the duty
of every officer and person in the employ or service of the City and County,
when it shall come to his knowledge that any contract or agreement with the

City and County, or with any officer or department thereof, or relating to the business of any office, has been or is about to be violated by the other contracting party, forthwith to report to the Mayor all facts and information within his possession concerning such matter. A wilful failure to do so shall be cause for the removal of such officer or employee. The Mayor shall give a certificate on demand to any person reporting such facts and information that he has done so, and such certificate shall be evidence in exoneration from a charge of neglect of duty.

The Mayor must institute such actions or proceedings as may be necessary to revoke, cancel or annul all franchises that may have been granted by the City and County to any person, company or corporation which have been forfeited in whole or in part or which for any reason are illegal and void and not binding upon the City. The City Attorney, on demand of the Mayor, must institute and prosecute the necessary actions to enforce the provisions of this section.

The Mayor shall have power to postpone final action on any franchise that may be passed by the Supervisors until such proposed franchise shall be ratified or rejected by a majority of the votes cast on the question at the next election.

Offices and Vacancies Not Provided in Charter.

Sec. 4. The Mayor shall appoint all officers of the City and County whose election or appointment is not otherwise specially provided for in this Charter or by law. When a vacancy occurs in any office, and provision is not otherwise made in this Charter or by law for filling the same, the Mayor shall appoint a suitable person to fill such vacancy, who shall hold office for the remainder of the unexpired term.

Ex-Officio President of Supervisors.

Sec. 5. The Mayor shall be President of the Board of Supervisors by virtue of his office. He may call extra sessions of the Board, and shall communicate to them in writing the objects for which they have been convened; and their acts at such sessions shall be confined to such objects.

President Pro Tem. Vacancy in Mayoralty.

Sec. 6. When and so long as the Mayor is temporarily unable to perform his duties, a member of the Board shall be chosen President pro tempore, who shall act as such Mayor. When a vacancy occurs in the office of Mayor, it shall be filled for the unexpired term by the Supervisors. . . .

ACQUISITION OF PUBLIC UTILITIES.

Intention of the People.

It is hereby declared to be the purpose and intention of the people of the City and County that its public utilities shall be gradually acquired and ultimately owned by the City and County. To this end it is hereby ordained:

Plans and Estimates of Cost of Construction. Cost of Water Works. Sources of Supply. Supervisors to Negotiate for Acquisition.

Section 1. Whenever the Board of Supervisors by ordinance, as hereinafter provided, shall determine that the public interest or necessity de-

mands the acquisition, construction or completion of any public utility or
utilities by the City and County, or whenever the electors shall petition
the Board of Supervisors, as provided in Section 3 of this Article, for the
acquisition of any public utility or utilities, the Board of Supervisors must
procure from the Board of Public Works, through the City Engineer, plans
and estimates of the cost of original construction and completion, by the
City and County, of such public utility or utilities.

In securing estimates of the cost of original construction and completion
of water works, by the City and County, the Board of Supervisors must procure, as hereinabove specified, and place on file plans and estimates of
the cost of obtaining from such sources as the Board of Supervisors may
designate as available, a sufficient supply of good, pure water for the City
and County. -- As amended December 4, 1920; approved by the Legislature
February 5, 1903 (Statutes, 1903, page 591).

Offers for the Sale of Utilities.

Sec. 2. Before submittting propositions to the electors for the acquisition by original construction or condemnation of public utilities, the Board
of Supervisors must solicit and consider offers for the sale to the City and
County of existing utilities, in order that the electors may have the benefit
of acquiring the same at the lowest possible cost thereof. -- As amended
December 4, 1902; approved by the Legislature February 5, 1903 (Statutes,
1903, page 591).

Petition of Electors. Duty of Supervisors. Duty of Clerk. Mayor May
Also Submit Proposition. Two Alternative Propositions. Supervisors May
Proceed at Once. Power of Supervisors.

Sec. 3. Whenever a petition or petitions, each signed by electors of the
City and County equal in number to fifteen per centum of all the votes cast
in the City and County at the last preceding general election, shall be presented to the Board of Supervisors, setting forth that the signers of such petition or petitions favor the acquisition of the public utility or utilities therein named, it shall be the duty of the Clerk of the Board of Supervisors to
immediately proceed to examine and verify the signature to such petition
or petitions, and to certify the result of such examination to the Board of
Supervisors. If the required number of signatures be found to be genuine,
the Clerk shall transmit to the Mayor an authentic copy of such petition or
petitions, without the signatures thereto.

Upon receiving a certificate of the Clerk that the petition or petitions contain the required number of genuine signatures, it shall be the duty of the
Board of Supervisors to procure, in the manner specified in Section 1 of this
Article, plans and estimates of the cost of original construction and completion of each public utility named in such petition or petitions.

Thereafter, the Board of Supervisors shall formulate for submission to
the electors of the City and County at a special election called for the purpose, a separate proposition for the acquisition of each public utility named
in such petition or petitions.

The Mayor shall also have the right to formulate and submit to the electors, at such special election, a proposition for the acquisition of each public utility named in such petition or petitions, separate from the proposition therefor formulated by the Board of Supervisors.

All propositions formulated under the provision of this Section shall be completed within six months after the filing of such petition or petitions.

Nothing in this Section shall be so construed as to prohibit the Board of Supervisors from responding to the aforesaid petition or petitions of the electors requesting the acquisition of any public utility or utilities by proceeding at once, without the submission of propositions to the electors as aforesaid, to pass an Ordinance declaring its determination, as provided in Section 5 of this Article, to acquire the same, and from proceeding thereafter to secure the acquisition thereof, as hereinafter provided. . . .

THE GREAT EARTHQUAKE, 1906

The first published account of the earthquake
appeared in The Evening Daily News. Its plant
was damaged, but working, and therefore able
to print a report of the disaster.

(Source: The Evening Daily News, April 18, 1906.)

San Francisco was practically demolished and totally paralyzed by the
earthquake, which commenced at 5:11 A.M. today and continued with terrific vigor for four minutes.

Great loss of life was caused by the collapse of buildings, and many people met a more cruel death by fire. Flames broke out in all portions of
the city.

The monetary loss caused by the earthquake, the fires which followed
it and the depreciation of values that will result will amount to hundreds of
millions of dollars.

The progress of San Francisco has received a check from which it will
probably taken many years to recover.

Thousands of men who went to bed wealthy last night awoke this morning
practically bankrupt.

The fury of the temblor was greater than any that has been known in the
history of the city.

The people are appalled, terror-stricken. Thousands, fearing a recurrence of the dreadful disaster, with results still more dire, are hastening
out of San Francisco.

Many heart-rending scenes have been enacted. Families are moving
their belongings helter-skelter, and moving aimlessly about, keeping in
the open.

The City Hall is a complete wreck. The walls surrounding the grand
dome have fallen, leaving only the skeleton frame work and the top of the
dome intact. Around all sides of the building the walls have crumbled, like
so many cards. The Receiving Hospital is buried.

The surgeons moved to the Mechanics' Pavilion, which today is a combined hospital and morgue. Dead and dying are brought in by autos, ambu-
lances, and even garbage carts.

Insane patients were taken from the Emergency Hospital to the Mechanics' Pavilion. Many of them were hurt. Some broke loose and ran among
the dying, adding horror to the scene.

At 8:15 a second sharp quake occurred, accentuating the terror.

The fire scenes following the earthquake were and are fearful to behold.
Had the earthquake occurred an hour later, the entire city would have burst
into flame.

At least forty buildings were aflame within ten minutes after the temblor passed. Among the first to go were the big buildings on Market, Battery, Sansome, First, Second, Third, Fourth, Fifth and Sixth streets, followed by a general conflagration on Seventh and Eighth streets, while in the Western Addition many fires were started.

By eight o'clock it seemed that a large part of the city was doomed.

NEW YORK TIMES REPORT OF THE EARTHQUAKE

The horror and devastation of the earthquake can
best be told by the article which appeared in the
New York Times of April 19, 1906.

(Source: New York Times, April 19, 1906.)

SAN FRANCISCO, April 18. Earthquake and fire to-day have put nearly half of San Francisco in ruins. About 500 persons have been killed, a
thousand injured, and the property loss will exceed $300,000,000.

Fifty thousand people are homeless and destitute, and all day long
streams of people have been fleeing from the stricken districts to places of
safety.

It was 5:13 this morning when a terrific earthquake shock shook the
whole city and surrounding country. One shock apparently lasted two minutes, and there was almost immediate collapse of flimsy structures all
over the city.

The water supply was cut off, and when fires started in various sections there was nothing to do but let the buildings burn. Telegraph and telephone communication was cut off for a time.

Electric power was stopped and street cars did not run, railroads and
ferry boats ceased operations. The various fires raged all day and the
fire department has been powerless to do anything except dynamite buildings threatened. All day long explosions have shaken the city and added to
the terror of the inhabitants.

Following the first shock, there was another within five minutes but
not nearly so severe. Three hours later there was another slight quake.

First Warning at 5:13 A.M.

Most of the people of San Francisco were asleep at 5:13 o'clock this
morning when the terrible earthquake came without warning. The motion
of the disturbance apparently was from east to west. At first the upheaval
of the earth was gradual, but in a few seconds it increased in intensity.
Chimneys began to fall and buildings to crack, tottering on their founda-
tions.

The people became panic-stricken and rushed into the streets, most
of them in their night attire. They were met by showers of falling bricks,
cornices and walls of buildings.

Many were crushed to death, while others were badly mangled. Those
who remained indoors generally escaped with their lives, though scores
were hit by detached plaster, pictures, and articles thrown to the floor by
the shock. It is believed that more or less loss was sustained by nearly
every family in the city.

Steel Frame Buildings Stand.

The tall, steel-framed structures stood the strain better than brick
buildings, few of them being badly damaged. The big eleven-story Monad-

nock office building, in course of construction adjoining the Palace Hotel, was an exception, however, its rear wall collapsing and many cracks being made across its front.

Some of the docks and freight sheds along the water front slid into the bay. Deep fissures opened in the filled-in ground near the shore and the Union Ferry Station was badly injured. Its high tower still stands but will have to be torn down.

A portion of the new City Hall, which cost more than $7,000,000, collapsed, the roof sliding into the courtyard, and the smaller towers tumbling down. The great dome was moved but did not fall.

The new Post Office, one of the finest in the United States, was badly shattered.

The Valencia Hotel, a four-story wooden building, sank into the basement, a pile of splintered timbers, under which were pinned many dead and dying occupants of the house. The basement was full of water, and some of the helpless victims were drowned.

Fires Start in Many Places.

Scarcely had the earth ceased to shake when fires started simultaneously in many places. The Fire Department promptly responded to the first calls for aid, but it was found that the water mains had been rendered useless by the underground movement.

Fanned by a light breeze, the flames quickly spread, and soon many blocks were seen to be doomed. Then dynamite was resorted to, and the sound of frequent explosions added to the terror of the people. These efforts to stay the progress of the fire, however, proved futile.

The south side of Market Street, from Ninth Street to the bay, was seen ablaze, the fire covering a belt two blocks wide. On this, the main thoroughfare, were many of the finest edifices in the city including the Green Parrott, Call, Examiner and Monadnock Buildings and the Palace and Grand Hotels.

At the same time commercial establishments and banks north of Market Street were burning. The fire burned in this section of the city from Sansome Street to the waterfront and from Market Street to Broadway. Fires also started in the Mission and the entire city seemed to be in flames.

Long Detours Around Fires.

The flames, fanned by the rising breeze, swept down the main streets until within a few hundred feet of the ferry station, the high tower of which stood at a dangerous angle.

The big wholesale grocery establishment of Westman, Peck & Co. was on fire from cellar to roof, and the heat was so oppressive that passengers from the ferry boats were obliged to keep close to the water's edge in order to get past the burning structure.

It was impossible to reach the centre of the city from the bay without skirting the shore for a long distance so as to get entirely around the burning district.

About 8 o'clock the Southern Pacific officials refused to allow any more passengers from trans-bay points to land, and sent back those already on

the boats. The ferry and train service of the Key Route was entirely abandoned owing to damage done to the power house by the earthquake at Emery-
ville.

Lack of Dynamite Felt.

There was little dynamite available in the city. The Southern Pacific
soon brought some in. At 9 o'clock Mayor Schmitz sent a tug to Pinola for
several cases of explosives. He sent also a telegram to Mayor Mott of Oakland. At 10:30 he received this reply to his Oakland message:

"Three engines and hose companies leave here immediately. Will forward dynamite as soon as obtainable."

The town of San Rafael, despite its own needs sent fire fighting apparatus here.

Mayor Schmitz gave orders to dynamite wherever necessary, and the
firemen and United States soldiers, who assisted them, blew down building
after building. Their efforts, however, were useless, so far as checking
the headway of the flames was concerned.

The shortage of water was due to the breaking of the mains of the Spring
Valley Water Company at San Mateo. The water needed so badly in the city
ran in a flood over San Mateo.

Burning of the Opera House.

The fire swept down the streets so rapidly that it was practically impossible to save anything in its way. It reached the Grand Opera House
on Mission Street, and in a moment had burned through the roof. The Metropolitan Opera Company from New York had just opened its season there,
and all the expensive scenery and costumes were soon reduced to ashes.

From the opera house the fire leaped from building to building, levelling
them almost to the ground in quick succession.

The Call editorial and mechanical departments, in the handsome building
at Third and Market Streets, were totally destroyed in a few minutes, and
the flames leaped across Stevenson Street toward the fine fifteen-story
stone and iron building of Claus Spreckels, which, with its lofty domes,
was the most notable structure in San Francisco. Two small wooden buildings furnished fuel to ignite the spendid pile. Thousands of people watched
the hungry tongues of flames licking the stone walls. At first no impression was made, but suddenly there was a cracking of glass and an entrance
was effected. The inner furnishings of the fourth floor were the first to go.
Then, as if by magic, smoke issued from the top of the dome.

This was followed by a most spectacular illumination. The round windows of the dome shone like so many full-moons; they burst and gave vent
to long, waving streamers of flames. The crowd watched the spectacle
with bated breath. One woman wrung her hands and burst into a torrent of
tears. "It is so terrible," she said.

PROCLAMATION BY THE MAYOR
PLACING THE CITY UNDER MARTIAL LAW, 1906

(Source: New York Times, April 19, 1906.)

To the Citizens of San Francisco:

The Federal troops, which are now policing a portion of the city, as
well as the regular and special members of the police force, have been
authorized by me to kill any persons whomsoever found engaged in looting
the effects of any citizens or otherwise engaged in the commission of crime.

Under these circumstanes, they request that all citizens whose business
does not require their absence from home after dark, remain at home during the night time until order shall have been restored.

I have directed all the Gas and Electric Lighting Companies not to turn
on gas or electricity until I order them to do so; you may therefore expect
the city to remain in darkness for an indefinite time.

I warn all citizens of the danger of fire from damaged or destroyed chimneys, broken or leaking gas pipes or fixtures, or any like cause.

E. E. Schmitz, Mayor

BUBONIC PLAGUE, 1907

> In the fall of 1907, bubonic plague broke out
> in the city. The health officials reasoned that
> since the plague was spread by rats, to elimi-
> nate the plague, one had to eliminate the rat
> population in the city. Thus developed the
> greatest rat hunt in history. The following
> document is one of 700,000 pieces of printed
> instructions issued by the Citizens' Health
> Committee.

(Source: Citizens' Health Committee, Report, 1907.)

FASTEN THIS UP IN YOUR KITCHEN

Citizens' Health Committee,
Headquarters, Room 1233 Merchants' Exchange.

TO GET RID OF RATS.

KITCHEN RULES.

Keep all supplies in rat-proof bins.
Keep meats in safes or in refrigerators.
Keep uncooked vegetables in crates on shelves. Never on the floor.
   IF COOKING IS DONE WITH A COAL FIRE.
   Burn in your kitchen fire all refuse (trimmings of meat, bones, parings
of vegetables, eggshells, all platter and plate scrapings, and all waste food
food) as it occurs. This means the putting into the fire of small amounts
at a time, when they will readily burn. This is known to be a practical me-
thod. By it there is no garbage.
   IF COOKING IS DONE WITH A GAS FIRE.
Keep all garbage in covered metal cans..
Keep the cans closely covered.
Have the garbage removed at least twice a week.
Have scavenger carry your garbage can to his wagon.
Report all scavengers who do not do so.
Don't put garbage in slop hoopers.
Always clean up your own premises.
Throw no garbage into the street nor on vacant lots.
Admit authorized Health Inspectors to your premises. They are there for
your benefit.
Tell your neighbors to do all the above--and see that they do.

Report to the Committee all cases of insanitary conditions. These rules
to be in force during the existence of plague and afterwards.

THE BREAKING OF THE UNIONS, 1916

The spirit of the vigilantes was still present in San Francisco in 1916 when they got involved in one of the periodic labor disputes. During a strike of longshoremen which expanded to paralyze the entire city, violence erupted. The San Francisco merchants and citizens formed the Industrial Law and Order Committee. Aside from maintaining law and order, the committee's purpose was to destroy the unions by insuring an open shop policy. The following article is a description of the strike, how the committee broke it, and the anti-union sentiment in the country that led many cities to settle labor disputes by the San Francisco model.

(Source: The New York Times, March 25, 1917.)

San Francisco has a prescription that it earnestly recommends to the rest of the country. It is a prescription for a complaint from which the entire nation is suffering severely and for which many communities are anxiously seeking a remedy -- LABOR TROUBLE. The cures that are being suggested and even tried are elaborate concoctions with many of their ingredients taken from the pharmacopoeia of socialism, communism, and other popular sources. San Francisco's prescription is a plain, old-fashioned remedy. Here it is: "Enforce the law."

And San Francisco backs its prescription with a thought-compelling testimonial. It tells us that it was a sadly ailing patient: that its commercial life had been brought almost to a condition of absolute paralysis by a high-handed labor organization using the familiar methods of violence and intimidation -- a labor organization so high-handed and so all-powerful that during the strike that it waged it actually issued to the United States Sub-Treasurer permits for teams hauling bullion to the United States Treasury, to "pass through all picket lines."

Then, suddenly, the citizens met; a Law and Order Committee was formed; a million-dollar fund was raised for its use. But the most potent asset of the new Law and Order Committee was the fact that the sentiment of the great law-abiding section of the community was awakened and given an opportunity to focus itself into an active, aggressive force. It was a revival of the grim, determined spirit of the old Vigilantes -- the law was to be enforced without fear or favor, without refard to price.

Then late last Spring came the particular act of tyranny that played the part of the proverbial last straw.

The longshoremen's union and the employers had signed an agreement, one of the clauses of which provided that its terms should continue in effect until either party gave a sixty days' notice in writing of a desire to have those terms changed. On May 19, 1916, following the convention at Seattle of the longshoremen of the Pacific Coast, a letter was sent to the employers announcing that on June 1 a new schedule of wages and hours would be put in effect by the longshoremen.

Now, in addition to wages and hours, there were certain matters that it was imperative to settle with the union. For one thing, the labor autocracy was enforcing its ukase that no goods in any way tainted by nonunionism would be handled. Witness, for instance, the cargo of sugar which arrived at the docks in San Francisco and which was refused loading by the longshoremen because it had been handled by nonunion men en route. Another case concerned a large shipment of shingles, which was refused because it was assumed that the shingles had been made in an open-shop mill back in the mountains. Of course the transportation companies, as common carriers, were required by both State and Federal statute to receive and deliver these consignments.

Efforts by the employers to secure a conference before June 1 were frustrated by the longshoremen, and on June 1, the employers not having met the demands, a walkout occurred. . . .

Entirely aside from the loss to the paralyzed industries of the community, it is estimated that there was over two and a half million dollars worth of exports held up in June by the strike. The fact that 60 per cent of this freight was interstate and subject to Federal jurisdiction had no effect.

This, however, was not the only strike that was disturbing the industrial life and the civic peace of San Francisco at this time.

The lumber dealers and steam schooner owners had also received abrupt notice, in spite of a sixty-day contract clause, that they must immediately raise wages. The reply that business conditions did not permit of a raise in wages was swept aside. And on June 1 the Retail Lumber Dealers Association closed down their plants.

The owners of steamboats engaged in the bay and river trade also received a union command for an increase in wages. The owners offered to prove by their books that it would be impossible to pay this increase. The offer was refused. On June 1 the demands of the union became effective. In spite of the fact that for fourteen years there had been an understanding in this business that men would not be taken off a steamer until a cargo loaded in good faith, was unloaded, the firemen and deckhands were taken off four steamers that were about ready to cast off, tying up passengers and freight.

The San Francisco Building Trades Council sent notice to all structural steel firms that on and after July 10 structural steel workers, who had been working a nine-hour day, would only work an eight-hour day for nine hours' pay. The employers offered their books as evidence that conditions in San Francisco, also the competitive trade conditions with Eastern manufacturer, did not justify the demand. On July 10 the structural steel workers went on strike.

While these strikes were being called one after the other, another strike was being formented. The cooks, helpers, and waiters notified the restaurant men that on July 15 they would put into effect an eight-hour day at the prevailing wages. The employers offered a reduction of one hour in the working day at the same scale of wages. This compromise was rejected. The employers were asked to arbitrate and agreed on condition that the discussion of wages and hours be held on a basis of wages and hours prevailing in fifteen cities of the United States. This proposal was rejected, and on Aug. 1 a strike was called.

Acute disturbance in so many and such widespread industries caused a responding disturbance, both physical and psychologic, in every industry in the community -- there was not an activity that was not cramped -- dissatisfaction and disorder were in the air.

The labor autocrats immediately resorted to thuggery and terrorism. The police and hospital records of the period tell a graphic story of lawlessness. There was one killing. The facts that led up to this give us a vivid picture of longshore life in Frisco during this reign of terror.

Two nights before the killing, a strikebreaker named Hawkins, an American citizen, 60 years of age, living on a barge with other strike-breakers and engaged in loading and discharging cargo, left Pier 32 to make purchases in a store. He was set upon by a number of union pickets and taken to the headquarters of the longshoremen's union. The officers of the union catechised Hawkins at length, and then ostensibly ordered the pickets to see that he reached a street car in safety.

An hour or two later he was found by the police on East Street, so badly beaten that he was almost unrecognizable. He was unconscious, his body and head bruised from kicks and blows. The police took him to the barge instead of to the Emergency Hospital, and all of the 250 men living on the barge had an opportunity to see him -- an object lesson as to what would likely happen to any of them who ventured upon the streets.

Two nights later two negro strikebreakers left the pier in the same way and at the same place that Hawkins did. They were set upon by four pickets. One of the negroes shot and killed one of the pickets. The negro was arrested, charged with murder.

When this reign of violence began, a large committee of representative men waited upon the Mayor with whom were the President of the Police Commission and the Chief of Police. Positive assurance was given that there would be ample police protection; that law and order would be maintained, and that the regularly constituted authorities, without assistance, could guarantee protection.

The record of lawlessness shows the value of this official guarantee. . . .

But violence and lawlessness continued. Cartage to the waterfront continued to be a dangerous, almost a forbidden, occupation to any one who was not supplied with a pass from Murphy.

Outraged public opinion at last found expression. On July 6 the Chamber of Commerce, through its President, Frederick J. Koster, issued a call to the men of San Francisco.

The response was instant and electric. On July 10, 2,000 business and professional men crowded upon the floor of the Chamber of Commerce. The spirit and the purpose of the meeting are plainly set forth in this paragraph from the speech of President Koster:

"Gentlemen, we are here for a very serious purpose. This meeting must result in action made necessary by a condition which the business community cannot and must not tolerate any longer. We don't intend leaning upon any one on the outside in this matter -- we are going to do the job ourselves and do it thoroughly. Any one here who is not in the frame of mind where he will be prepared to do his full duty, and who cannot be counted on for loyalty and determination, would best quietly and promptly leave this meeting."

It was resolved that President Koster appoint a Law and Order Committee of five, including himself as Chairman, "with full power to act."

Within five minutes after the organization of the committee $200,000 had been voluntarily subscribed for its work. Within a week this was increased to $600,000, and soon thereafter the fund reached, in round figure, $1,000,000. That the law-abiding element only needed leadership, only needed something to rally around, is shown by the fact that the membership of the Chamber jumped from 2,400 to 6,313, making it the largest Chamber of Commerce in the United States.

One of the first decisions of the Law and Order Committee was that if the draymen and teamsters were unwilling or powerless to act, freight would be moved to and from the terrorized waterfront willy-nilly. To this end the committee obtained from the business houses of San Francisco powers of attorney to make or cancel draying contracts.

But these powers of attorney were never used: THE FREIGHT MOVED. The voice of righteousness -- with force at its command -- had spoken , and the evil spell that had been cast over San Francisco was broken.

On July 17 the longshoremen returned to work under conditions prevailing when the walkout took place on June 1, but with the understanding that a conference of employer and employees would be held on Aug. 1. This conference resulted in an agreement under which the employer agreed to hire members of the union when available, and the union members agreed to do all work and handle all freight without any question as to whether or not it was "tainted" by nonunion labor. An increase of wages was granted. This was done because the union controlled the greater part of the skilled longshore labor and it could, therefore, collectively negotiate for price under the time-honored, law-sanctioned rules of the market place.

Meanwhile the strike on the steamboats engaged in the bay and river trade collapsed completely. The open shop rule was established. Many of the strikers returned to work, positions being provided for as many as possible. Wherever vacancies occur, former employees are taken back without prejudice.

Then came the blow from ambush -- the terrible culmination of San Francisco's long period of lawlessness. On Preparedness Day, July 22, a bomb was exploded at Stewart and Market Streets while the parade was passing. Ten men and women were killed and fifty injured.

The Law and Order Committee immediately met, and it was determined that the public should be given an opportunity to express its condemnation of the outrage. A mass meeting was called for the night of July 26. The committee received a letter threatening that if this meeting was held another bomb would be exploded and that a greater toll of life would be taken than on Preparedness Day. This letter was in the same handwriting as the letters which had been received by the newspapers forewarning them of the Preparedness Day outrage.

Six thousand men and women braved that threat. The mass meeting was a solemn and impressive gathering that testified to the inflexibility of purpose with which San Francisco had set about the work of redeeming the city from anarchy. The public authorities could not mistake the voice with which this mass meeting commanded them to hunt down the assassins.

Notorious dynamiters, some of whom have had official connection with organized labor, were arrested and indicted for this crime. One of them has already been convicted and sentenced to life imprisonment. The men arrested were ferreted out by city officials sympathetic with labor organizations but spurred to activity by an outraged public opinion. It is a matter of some significance that the State Labor Council publicly pledged its support to the men arrested for this crime.

Two days after the mass meeting the structural steel operators declared for the open shop. On the same day the lumbermen opened their yards again under open-shop conditions, employing without discrimination union or nonunion workmen. And a few days later, when the culinary crafts went on strike, the restaurant men also declared for the open shop.

This last strike was attended by some little violence and by disorder of a very objectionable sort. The violence was no longer open and defiant as it was in the longshoremen's strike. It was not of a guerrilla character. There were scattered assaults by pickets. It was the disorderly conduct however, that in this strike was particularly offensive. Pickets used profane and indecent language in the hearing of the patrons, both men and women. There was disorderly conduct in front of the restaurants. Patrons were insulted as they went in or out. Then there were smuggled into the restaurants bombs which, when stepped on, released evil-smelling fumes of such potency that diners were driven out of doors.

The Law and Order Committee decided that picketing is a constant source of friction which often develops into violence, that it is an invasion of the rights of the employer, of his customers, and of those who want to work for him. The committee decided that the picket had to go.

Sufficient signatures were secured to an initiative petition putting an anti-picketing ordinance upon the ballot on Nov. 7. A campaign of publicity was inaugurated by the publication in every paper in the city of the record of violence that was a direct outgrowth of picketing. Every voter was appealed to by letter. Handbills were distributed. The climax of this campaign came on Nov. 4 and 6, when, with the aid of 400 telephone girls working in two shifts, every man and woman in San Francisco who could be reached by telephone was called up and urged to "vote yes on Ordinance 8 and prohibit picketing."

On election day the picket was banished from San Francisco.

On Nov. 22 the lumber handlers voted to return to work, under the former schedule of hours and wages, but under open-shop conditions.

On Dec. 16 the culinary crafts called their strike off.

San Francisco was an open-shop city.

THE PAGODA-LIKE PHONE EXCHANGE, 1929

San Francisco's Chinatown did not always have the oriental flavor that is so familiar today. The major reason for its present character was the construction of the telephone company along oriental lines.

(Source: The New York Times, March 10, 1929.)

SAN FRANCISCO CHINATOWN HAS A PAGODA-LIKE PHONE EXCHANGE

Perhaps the most unique telephone exchange in the United States is is Chinatown, San Francisco. There are many peculiar features about the China exchange. The building is of Chinese design, with a three-pagoda roof, the exterior painted in green, red and black; the interior in black, Chinese red and gilt. Beautifully colored glass lanterns hang from the ceiling.

As the Chinese have no alphabet, the Chinese telephone directory is arranged by streets, the name of the street appearing across the top of the page. At the left of the column is the telephone number, then the name of the subscriber, then the street number. The Chinese Subscribers do not call by number but by name, therefore the operators must memorize the names of all the subscribers - approximately 2,500. Frequently, it happens that there is more than one person with the same name, in which case the operator must secure some identification of the person called. If a call comes for "Chan Wing," and there is more than one Chan Wing on the list, the operator will say, "Which Chan Wing you want?" "The Grocer on the corner," comes the reply, and so the operator is able to call the right Chan Wing. Furthermore, she must speak four dialects, but that is not considered an unusual accomplishment.

There is very little turnover in the personnel at the exchange. One of the operators, who is completing her twenty-third year of service, has her young daughter sitting by her side employed in a similar capacity. The manager, who was trained under his father, the founder and manager for thirty-two years, is a young Chinese and is a native of Chinatown.

CITY CHARTER OF 1931

This charter was designed to correct the deficiencies in the charter of 1900 by which Boss Ruef and Mayor Schmitz were able to control the city.

The new charter tried to correct these difficulties by separating legislative and administrative functions. It combined a strong mayor with a city manager, each in control of different departments. Some of the provisions of this charter follow.

(Source: San Francisco City Charter, 1931.)

These provisions are pertinent:

Except for the purpose of inquiry, each board or commission, in its conduct of administrative affairs under its control, shall deal with such matters solely through its chief executive officer.

. . .The board of supervisors, and each board or commission relative to the affairs of its own department, shall deal with administrative matters only in the manner provided by this charter, and any dictation, suggestion or interference herein prohibited on the part of any supervisor or member of a board or commission shall constitute official misconduct provided, however, that nothing herein contained shall restrict the power of hearing and inquiry as provided in this charter.

No member of any board or commission shall accept any employment relating to the business or the affairs of any person, firm or corporation which are subject to regulation by the board or commission of which he is a member. . . .Violation of any of the provisions of this section shall constitute official misconduct.

Any person found guilty of official misconduct shall forfeit his office, and shall be forever after debarred and disqualified from being elected, appointed or employed in the service of the city and county.

Except for the purpose of inquiry, the mayor and the board of supervisors shall deal with the administrative service for which the chief administrative officer is responsible, solely through such officer, and for administrative or other functions for which elective officials or boards or commissions are responsible, solely through the elective official, the board or commission or the chief executive officer of such board or commission concerned. . . .

Neither the board of supervisors, nor its committees, nor any of its members shall dictate, suggest or interfere with appointments, promotions, compensations, disciplinary actions, contracts, requisitions for purchases or other administrative recommendations or actions of the chief administrative officer, or of department heads under the chief administrative officer, or under the respective boards and commissions. The board of supervisors, and each board or commission relative to the affairs of its own department, shall deal with administrative matters only in the manner provided by this charter, and any dictation, suggestion or interference herein prohibited on the part of any supervisor or member of a board or commission shall constitute official misconduct; provided, however, that nothing herein contained shall restrict the power of hearing and inquiry as provided in this charter.

The city and county may make and enforce all laws, ordinances and regulations necessary, convenient or incidental to the exercise of all rights and powers in respect to its affairs, officers, and employees, and shall have all rights and powers appropriate to a county, a city, and a city and county, subject only to the restrictions and limitations provided in this charter, including the power to acquire and construct plants, works, utilities, areas, highways and institutions outside the boundaries of the city and county, and maintenance and operation of the same. . . .The exercise of all rights and powers of the city and county when not prescribed in this charter shall be as provided by ordinance or resolution of the board of supervisors.

Powers of the city and county, except the powers reserved to the people or delegated to other officials, boards or commissions by this charter shall be vested in the board of supervisors and shall be exercised as provided in this charter. The board of supervisors shall, ex-officio, be the board of equalization for the city and county. It shall be the duty of the board of supervisors to canvass the vote cast at each election in the city and county, and certify the official count of such balloting. The supervisors shall determine the maximum number of each class of employments in each of the various departments and offices of the city and county and shall fix rates and schedules of compensation therefor in the manner provided in this charter. On the recommendation of the mayor and the chief administrative officer, the board of supervisors may create or abolish departments which are now or may hereafter be placed under the chief administrative officer or under commissions appointed by the mayor.

The board of supervisors may, by ordinance, confer on any officer, board or commission such other and additional powers as the board may deem advisable.

The board of supervisors may decrease or reject any item contained in the budget estimates, but shall not increase any amount or add any new item for personal services or materials, supplies, or contractual services for any department, unless requested in writing so to do by the mayor, on the recommendation of the chief administrative officer, board, commission or elective officer, in charge of such department.

The purchaser of supplies shall establish specifications and tests to cover all recurring purchases of material, supplies and equipment. He shall, as far as is practicable, standardize materials, supplies and equipment according to the use to which they are to be put, when two or more types, brands or kinds are specified or requested by individual departments.

Purchases of equipment shall be made in accordance with specifications furnished by the department requiring such equipment in case the use of such equipment is peculiar to such department. For patented or proprietary articles sold by brand name, the purchaser may require each department requisitioning same by such brand name, to furnish specifications of the article requisitioned and may advertise for bids on the basis of such specifications, under conditions permitting manufacturers of or dealers in other articles made and sold for the same purpose to bid on such specifications or on the specifications of their own product. . .

The purchaser of supplies shall require departments to make adequate inspection of all purchases, and shall make such other inspection as he deems necessary. . . .

He shall have charge of central storerooms and warehouses of the city and county. . . .

All contracts of purchase shall be made after inviting sealed bids by publication.

Appropriations for material, supplies, and equipment shall be segregated in each annual appropriation ordinance for each department or office. Any part of each such fund or appropriation may, on the recommendation of the purchaser of supplies and the approval of the controller, be transferred to or made available in the purchaser's revolving fund. Warrants shall be drawn against such fund by the controller on demand of the purchaser for the payment of bills on which discount for prompt payment may be secured, or for advantageous cash purchasing, under favorable or emergency market conditions, of materials or supplies for future departmental requisition and use. Discounts obtained by the use of the purchaser's revolving fund may be accumulated therein and the supervisors may make annual appropriations to such fund until a sufficient sum, as determined by the controller, is accumulated to meet the average purchasing and discount payment requirements of the city and county.

The construction, reconstruction or repair of public buildings, streets, utilities or other public works or improvements, and the purchasing of supplies, materials and equipment, when the expenditure involved in each case shall exceed the sum of one thousand dollars ($1,000.00), shall be done by contract, except as otherwise provided by this charter. It shall constitute official misconduct to split or divide any public work or improvement or purchase into two or more units for the purpose of evading the contract provisions of this section. . . .

Any public work or improvement estimated to cost less than one thousand dollars ($1,000.00)may be performed under contract or written order or by the employment of the necessary labor and purchase of the necessary materials and supplies directly by the city and county. Any public work or improvement executed by the city, other than routine repair work, shall be authorized by the chief administrative officer or by the heads of departments not under the chief administrative officer, only after detailed estimates have been prepared and submitted by the head of the department concerned. . . .

The board of supervisors, by ordinance, shall establish procedure whereby appropriate city and county departments may file sealed bids for the execution of any work to be performed under contract. If such bid is the lowest, the contract shall be awarded to the department. Accurate unit costs shall be kept of all direct and indirect charges incurred by the department under any such contract, which unit costs shall be reported to and audited by the controller monthly and on the completion of the work.

The commission shall have power to fix, change and adjust rates, charges or fares for the furnishing of service by any utility under its jurisdiction, and to collect by appropriate means all amounts due for said service, and to discontinue service to delinquent consumers and to settle and adjust claims arising out of the operation of any said utilities. . . .

Rates for each utility shall be so fixed that the revenue therefrom shall be sufficient to pay, for at least the succeeding fiscal year, all expenses of every kind and nature incident to the operation and maintenance of said utility, together with the interest and sinking fund for any bonds issued for the acquisition, construction or extension of said utility; provided that, should the commission propose a schedule of rates, charges or fares for said utility which shall not produce such revenue, it may do so with the approval of the board of supervisors, by a two-thirds vote and it shall thereupon be incumbent to provide by tax levy for the additional amount necessary to meet such deficit.

Active participation in city and county politics, relative to the election or appointment of public officials, by civil service employees and eligibles of the city and county, is subversive of the best interests of the merit system and, therefore, persons holding positions in the classified civil service or on eligible lists for such positions shall take no active part in such political campaigns, or in soliciting votes, or in levying, contributing or soliciting funds or support, in each case for the purpose of favoring or hindering the appointment or election of candidates for city and county offices. Violation of the provisions of this section shall be deemed an act of insubordination and considered good cause for suspension or dismissal from position or removal from eligible list. . . .

OPPOSITION TO THE 1931 CHARTER BY VESTED INTERESTS

There was strong opposition to the new charter by vested interests, and some city employees as this editorial in the Monitor illustrates.

(Source: Monitor, March 21, 1931.)

OFFICIAL OR UNOFFICIAL GOVERNMENT?

DISCUSSION OF CHARTER WHICH WOULD DEPRIVE VOTERS OF THEIR CONTROL OVER THE CITY AND COUNTY OF SAN FRANCISCO.

ADOPTION OF FREEHOLDERS' CHARTER WOULD LEGALIZE
AUTOCRACY

Editorial.

What is wrong with the Freeholder's Charter?. . . .The poor are liable to exploitation and degradation under the autocracy that the proposed charter would legalize. . . .

. . . The Freeholders' Charter would change the fundamental character of San Francisco by changing it from a democracy to an autocracy, by silencing political discussion, by enabling a few rich men to rule the City as medieval cities were ruled by merchant princes and bankers like the Medici. . . .

. . .The proposed Freeholders' Charter is really a rich men's scheme. Its origins recede into darker places than the innocent meetings of the late Board of Freeholders. Choking at the label 'City Manager,' the Freeholders were beguiled into accepting the same thing under the more novel label of 'Chief Administrative Officer.' . . .The functions of the proposed Chief Administrative Officer are like those of Stalin, the Dictator of Russia. . . .

Otherwise, it is a masterpiece of legal quackery. It is in its departmental details a melancholy exhibition of incompetent and destructive law-making. Though its provisions for the Police Department would expose the Police and all citizens to the rule of blackmail and intimidation, otherwise known as racketeering; though its provisions for the Fire Department, in respect of regulation of buildings would invite the bribery common in such matters in eastern cities; though Civil Service is made more of a farce than it now is and absolutely subjects civil servants to the spoils system; though the School Department is strengthened in its power to reject applicants undesirable to the incumbent executive for reasons not in the charter and though teachers are made more insecure in their tenure; though the Supervisors would be rendered less effective than they now are; though the Chief Administrative Officer would be tempted to graft and given ample opportunity to do so, though nearly every individual part of the proposed charter is full of loopholes (jokers), we prefer to discuss it as a whole.

As a whole the proposed charter is a franchise for autocracy. . . .

The way to prevent the deepest calamity and disgrace of San Francisco, the way to prevent the betrayal of the City into unlimited embarrassment and folly, the way to defend the citizens from the shameful robbery of their dignity and property, the way to show your abhorrence of the shocking and impious assumption that you are necessarily a fool is to vote 'No' on the Freeholders' Charter.

Under such a government as the proposed charter presents there would be no hope of religious liberty, freedom in education, free speech.

LABOR VIOLENCE, JULY 6, 1934

San Francisco has always had a history of labor troubles, but the bloodiest conflict occurred in 1934, when a general strike started on the waterfront and paralyzed the city. The document below describes the fifty-eighth day of the strike, the day chosen to test the strikers' power to stop the flow of goods.

(Source: San Francisco Chronicle, July 6, 1934.)

BLOODY THURSDAY

July 6, 1934

Blood ran red in the streets of San Francisco yesterday.

In the darkest day this city has known since April 18, 1906, one thousand embattled police held at bay five thousand longshoremen and their sympathizers in a sweeping front from south of Market street and east of Second street.

The furies of street warfare raged for hour piled on hour.

Two were dead, one was dying, 32 others shot and more than three score sent to hospitals.

Hundreds were injured or badly gassed. Still the strikers surged up and down the sunlit streets among thousands of foolhardy spectators. Still the clouds of tear gas, the very air darkened with hurtling bricks. Still the revolver battles.

As the middle of the day wore on in indescribable turmoil the savagery of the conflict was in rising crescendo. The milling mobs fought with greater desperation, knowing the troops were coming; the police held to hard-won territory with grim resolution.

It was a Gettysburg in the miniature, with towering warehouses thrown in for good measure. It was one of those days you think of as coming to Budapest.

The purpose of it all was this: The State of California has said it would operate its waterfront railroad. The strikers had defied the State of California to do it. The police had to keep them off. They did.

Take a San Francisco map and draw a line along Second street south from Market to the bay. It passes over Rincon Hill. That is the west boundary, Market is the north of the battlefield.

Not a street in that big sector but saw its flying lead yesterday, not a street that wasn't tramped by thousands of flying feet as the tide of battle swung high and low, as police drove them back, as they drove police back in momentary victory.

And with a dumfounding nonchalance, San Franciscans, just plain citizens bent on business, in automobiles and on foot, moved to and fro in the battle area.

Don't think of this as a riot. It was a hundred riots, big and little, first here, now there. Don't think of it as one battle, but as a dozen battles.

It started with a nice, easy swing just as great battles in war often start. The Industrial Association resumed moving goods from Pier 38 at 8 A.M. A few hundred strikers were out, but were held back at Brannan street, as they had been in Tuesday's riot, by the police.

At Bryant and Main streets were a couple of hundred strikers in an ugly mood. Police Captain Arthur de Guire decided to clear them out, and his men went at them with tear gas. The strikers ran, scrambling up Rincon Hill and hurling back rocks.

Proceed now one block away, to Harrison and Main streets. Four policemen are there, about 500 of the mob are on the hill. Those cops looked like fair game.

"Come on, boys," shouted the leaders.

They tell how the lads of the Confederacy had a war whoop that was a holy terror. These boys, a lot of them kids in their teens, came down that hill with a whoop. It sounded blood-curdling. One policeman stood behind a telephone pole to shelter him from the rocks and started firing with his revolver.

Up the hill, up Main, came de Guire's men on the run, afoot and the "mounties." A few shots started whizzing from up the hill, just a scattering few, with a high hum like a bumble bee.

Then de Guire's men, about 20 of them, unlimbered from Main and Harrison and fired at random up the hill. The down-plunging mob halted, hesitated, and started scrambling up the hill again.

Clatter, clatter, clatter come the bricks. Tinkle goes a window. This is war, boys, and this Steuart street between Howard and Mission is one of the warmest spots American industrial conflict ever saw.

The horses rear. The mounted police dodge bricks.

A police gold braid stands in the middle of the street all alone, and he blows his whistle. Up come the gas men, the shotgun men, the rifle men. The rioters don't give way.

Crack and boom! Sounds just like gas bomb, but no blue smoke this time. Back scrambles the mob and two men lie on the sidewalk. Their blood trickles in a crimson stream away from their bodies.

Over it all spreads an air of unutterable confusion. The only organization seems to lie in little squads of officers hurrying hither and yon in automobiles. Sirens keep up a continual screaming in the streets. You can hear them far away.

Now it was 2 o'clock. The street battle had gone on for half an hour. How many were shot, no one knew.

Now, it was win or die for the strikers in the next few hours. The time from 2 o'clock to 3 o'clock dragged for police, but went on the wings of the wind for the strikers. An hour's rest. They had to have that one hour.

At 3 o'clock they started again, the fighting surging once more about Steuart and Mission streets. Here was a corner the police had, and had to hold. It was the key to the waterfront, and it was in the shadow of I.L.A. headquarters.

The rocks started filling the air again. They crashed through street cars. The cars stopped and citizens huddled inside.

Panic gripped the east end of Market street. The ferry crowds were being involved. You thought again of Budapest. The troops were coming. Soldiers. SOLDIERS IN SAN FRANCISCO! WAR IN SAN FRANCISCO!

Here the first man fell, a curious bystander. The gunfire fell away.

Up came the tear gas boys, six or eight carloads of them. They hopped out with their masks on, and the gas guns laid down a barrage on the hillside. The hillside spouted blue gas like the Valley of the Ten Thousand Smokes.

Up the hill went the moppers-up, phalanxes of policemen with drawn revolvers. The strikers backed sullenly away on Harrison street, past Fremont street. Suddenly came half a dozen carloads of men from the Bureau of Inspectors, and right behind them a truck load of shotguns and ammunition.

In double quick they cleared Rincon Hill. Ten police cars stuck their noses over the brow of the hill.

Noon came. Napoleon said an army travels on its belly. So do strikers and police, and even newspapermen.

Now it is one o'clock. Rumors of the coming of the soldiery fly across the town. The strikers are massing down at the foot of Mission and Howard streets, where a Belt Line freight train is moving through.

Police massed there, too; the tear gas squads, the rifle and shotgun men, the mounties. Not a sign of machine guns so far. But the cops have them. There's plenty of talk about the "typewriters."

There they go again into action, the gas boys! They're going up the stubby little streets from the Embarcadero to Steuart street, half blocks up Mission and Howard. Across by the Ferry Building are thousands of spectators.

Boom! go the gas guns, boom, boom, boom!

Around corners, like sheep pouring through a gate, go the rioters, but they don't go very far. They stop at some distance, say a half block away, wipe their eyes a minute, and in a moment comes a barrage of rocks.

Here's the hottest part of the battle from now on, along Steuart street from Howard to Market. No mistake about that. It centers near the I.L.A. headquarters.

See the mounties ride up toward that front of strikers. It's massed across the street, a solid front of men. Take a pair of opera glasses and look at their faces. They are challenging the oncoming mounties. The men in front are kneeling, like sprinters at the mark.

RECOMMENDATIONS OF THE CITY PLANNING COMMITTEE, 1965

A two-year study of San Francisco was completed in 1965. The study noted that the city was starting to decline, and recommended a massive urban renewal project. A newspaper report of the study and its recommendations follow.

(Source: The New York Times, April 11, 1965.)

SAN FRANCISCO, April 10
-- The family is deserting San Francisco and is being replaced by the widow or widower, the bachelor and the working girl.

This was one of the conclusions reached in a two-year, $1 million study just completed, with the Federal Government paying two-thirds of the bill.

Arthur D. Little, Inc., management research consultants of Cambridge, Mass., made the survey. In their report this week to the City Planning Commission, the consultants recommended that San Francisco undertake the most extensive improvement program since the 1906 earthquake and fire.

The city learned some things about itself. Some paradoxes like this one were produced in the final report:

"In terms of families' with children, San Francisco, more than any other major city in America, has been a victim of the lure of the suburbs even though its percentage of locations suitable to families is probably greater than that of any other city in America."

Lowest in Nation

The investigators pointed to the city as suffering from a dearth of middle-income families, "traditionally the foundation of the economic and social structure of our society."

The study found that in 1960 families with children constituted only slightly more than 23 per cent of the total households in San Francisco, the lowest percentage of any major city in the country.

Despite the family's flight to "more desirable environmental amenities" the staff making the study came under the spell of San Francisco as "the embodiment of charm, beauty, culture and gracious living."

"It has developed this image," the report asserted, "by blending some of the finest attributes of the East and West Coasts within the framework of a cosmopolitan environment. . .to most people San Francisco symbolizes excitement and opportunity."

But the Little organization cautioned that the city was changing -- "partly because of national trends, partly from bay area trends and partly from San Francisco's own special quality."

"For example," it said, "like other urban areas throughout the country, San Francisco is losing manufacturing firms and employment to suburban areas and is experiencing an increase in low-income groups."

$45 Million Program

Regardless of this, Dr. Cyril C. Herrmann, a Little organization vice president who is responsible for work in city planning, declared that San Francisco "has the opportunity of surpassing all other cities in the quality of its buildings, its beauty and amenities, and its concern for the economic and social well-being of its citizens."

He said the action called for in the recommended community renewal program would cost $45 million over the next six years.

"Two thirds of this amount," he continued, "will come from the Federal Government. One third comes from the city. Through the use of capital improvements, such as streets, parks, schools and other needed improvements, the one-third input from the city need not involve any cash dedicated solely to renewal."

The analysis convinced the study staff that economic growth and development was an urgent need. The analysts found that manufacturing activities were dwindling and that the city's economy was becoming more and more dependent upon trade, services and finance, insurance and real estate. They said that efforts to upgrade San Francisco's physical plant must recognize this fact.

They found the housing supply in relatively good condition, with deterioration perhaps a serious problem at a future date, and they said that buildings and public officials should focus efforts on providing single-family, owner-occupied and rental structures. Many small apartment buildings would have to be upgraded.

The analysis put great emphasis on the design and operation of a programming computer that Dr. Herrmann asserted "is unique (and) places San Francisco in the forefront of planning activity in the United States."

The computer is described as giving a comprehensive forecast of changes that would occur in the city if certain actions were taken. Spokesmen for the Little organization said that costly mistakes thus could be avoided and the process of decision-making could be improved.

But, Dr. Hermann protested, "the city has not been turned over to a machine."

"The programming model doesn't make decisions in terms of telling you where to build the next building," he explained. "However, for an investor who is going to build in San Francisco, the model will provide him with more and better information to guide his own decision than has been available before."

THE HIPPIE SUBCULTURE, 1967

In the middle sixties, San Francisco, along with the East Village in New York, became the center of the counter-culture when a hippie community grew up in the Haight-Ashbury section of the city. At first, the city with its usual permissiveness accepted the flower children, but, as the writer of the article demonstrtes, not everyone in the city was tolerant. Even though the author, because of his prejudice, missed the significance of the movement, it is interesting for its view of the Haight-Ashbury scene of the sixties, and a prediction of things to come.

(Source: The New York Times, May 4, 1967.)

SAN FRANCISCO, April 30
-- The hippies are becoming more and more organized. They have two newspapers and a civic association.

If this trend continues the hippies won't be hippies anymore, hippie admirers feel, and this city's Haight-Ashbury section, the hippie capital, will turn into just another Bohemian quarter like North Beach here or East Village in New York.

Villagers are for things: non-involvement in Vietnam and Negro civil rights. Hippies are for nothing. "Why can't I stand on a street corner and wait for nobody? Why can't everyone?"

Or, as Claude Haywood, a married 21-year-old hippie with shoulder length hair, said, "The world is going to chew you up, so why bother? Just wait until it does." Mr. Haywood migrated here from New York four years ago.

Hippies almost always refer to Negroes as "spades."

They have no malicious intent, but they don't dig the civil rights movement. David Simpson, 26, a hippie who came here from Chicago four years ago, summed it up this way: "The Negroes are fighting to become what we've rejected. We don't see any sense in that."

Mr. Simpson, a college graduate, has nearly shoulder-length blond hair. He wears a large gold earring and around his head, a light blue cloth band. It holds in place on his forehead a stuffed parakeet -- the tail of which curls along the ridge of his nose. He calls himself "Bird" and is somewhat typical of the Haight-Ashbury hippies.

"We're trying various experiments in living. I'm getting a new pad. Nine of us will move in, and see how it works out," he explained.

Haight-Ashbury is a lower middle-class section of San Francisco. Its residences are mostly three- and four-story homes that have been converted into apartment houses, as the brownstones were converted in New York.

Most of the area's residents have learned to live with the 15,000 or so hippies for neighbors. But despite the hippies' almost total non-involvement there are some things hippies do actively like, and these bother not only their neighbors but the San Francisco police as well.

Hippies like LSD, marijuana, nude parties, sex, drawing on walls and sidewalks, not paying their rent, making noise and rock 'n' roll music.

Earlier this week, music was blasting from an apartment window overlooking the intersection of Haight (pronounced Hate) and Ashbury Streets. Before long, several hundred hippies were dancing to it in the street.

When the police arrived, the hippies, who are usually nonviolent, showered them with fruit and vegetables. About 50 of the hippies were rounded up and carted off in paddy wagons but all but 16 were let go.

There are two philosophical trends in hippiedom, and as the hippies become organized, those who adhere to one or the other hippie concept tend to become less tolerant of the other.

The old-line hippies are definitely religious in a general sense. "God is Love," is the basic tenet of their subculture. They whisper that to passersby on the street, are always calm and friendly, and they will demonstrate their love for humanity by throwing flowers at the police who harry them. Flowers and bells are their cross and crown.

These hippies publish a newspaper, The Oracle, which is illustrated with psychedelic pictures. It contains articles that feature no news, but essays on loving one another.

Younger hippies, however, have a slightly different "thing" or way of life, which was summed up by one of them this way: "Think what you want, but the number one rule is that you can't force your thing on other people."

They also operate a newspaper, the Communication Company, which publishes mimeographed tracts for the hippies.

The Communication Company was started in January and has already put out more than 500 communications. It operates out of the top floor of a three-story apartment, in which members of the staff smoke grass, or marijuana, take LSD trips together, and sleep on mattresses on littered floors.

The company has run out of rent money, so eviction proceedings have started. However, the company does own three mimeograph machines, an electronic copier and a hi-fi set.

"It will take two months before we go through the courts," one staff member said. "We'll have two months of free living. That's part of our thing anyhow. We're teaching people how to survive, be fed and clothed, without having any money."

Because the daily use of drugs is such a common part of life in Haight-Ashbury, one of the most popular items put out by the Communication Company is called "The Dope Sheet." It is a four-page, single-spaced text on how to use drugs, particularly LSD, and advises the hippies to take their first "trip" with "someone who is wiser and/or more experienced than you -- someone you trust, who should be able to answer whatever questions you may be able to ask."

The sheet notes that "one of the reasons hippies are so fond of (American) Indians is that acid (LSD) dissolves our European conditioning and turns us into temporary Indians."

This affinity for Indians is reflected in the style the hippies affect. Many wear ponchos. Bells and beads and even seeds around their necks are common. One young hippie from Westport, Conn., wears a bicycle chain around his neck. He has no home, but wanders nightly from place to place looking for an apartment to "crash" -- that is, sleep in.

All pure hippies, both boys and girls, have long and dirty hair. And though many of them work -- a number of them are postmen -- and have cars, they do not like to pay their bills, so often the water is shut off in their pads, making it difficult for them to wash.

The Haight-Ashbury hippies differ from residents of other Bohemian centers in that they have a strong communal sense. A number of them recently have formed what they call a "survival school." This was set up to teach young would-be hippies how to survive without money. Another group is called the Diggers, and it is the hippies' civic association.

The Diggers have set up a free store with racks and piles of used clothing that people can have free. It is not uncommon to see mothers outfitting their small children in the free store, being as picky and choosy among the dirty clothes and shoes as they would in a regular department store.

The Diggers also give out free luncheons -- mostly leftover food donated by nearby restaurants. People are encouraged to come into the free store and paint psychedelic pictures on their clothing or dance, or neck, or do anything they want.

The other day a small group of hippies was sitting around a coffin in the store discussing jazz.

While the hippies insist they love just about everyone, nobody here loves the hippies. But they have become a tourist attraction, and traffic jams are not uncommon in Haight-Ashbury as people drive slowly through the area gawking at the hippies, who have, for example, put dimes in the parking meters and lain in the parking space on the street.

One bus line has put on a daily tourist tour billed as the "Hippie Hop" through the "Sodom" of Haight-Ashbury.

The city fears a possible mass migration of would-be hippies to the area this summer from all over the country. The hippies themselves keep frightening the city establishment by predicting the 100,000 teenagers will flock here this summer to become hippies.

BIBLIOGRAPHY

The emphasis in this bibliography is to present a well rounded list of books from which the interested reader may obtain additional information. It contains source material, secondary historical works, and books about specific issues. It has been critically selected and includes works that, for the most part, are readily available to students. Additional titles may be found in the Harvard Guide to American History, Cambridge, 1954. For articles in scholarly journals, consult the Reader's Guide to Periodical Literature and the Social Sciences and Humanities Index.

It should also be noted that the most important source for material on the history of San Francisco is the Bancroft Collection located at the University of California at Berkeley. Aside from containing the world's largest collection of books and documents on San Francisco, it houses a huge collection of material relating to California and the American West. Surprisingly, it is also valuable for collateral areas such as Spanish America, and the European background to American Colonization.

BIBLIOGRAPHY

Anon. "Filings from an Old Saw," The Golden Era, 1852. San Francisco, 1930. Lively first-hand account of San Francisco in the 1850's which appeared in a weekly newspaper.

Anson, Lord. A Voyage Round the World. London, 1911.

Ashbury, Herbert. The Barbary Coast: An Informal History of the San Francisco Underworld. New York, 1933.

Atherton, Gertrude. California, an Intimate History. New York, 1914.

------------------. Golden Gate Country. New York, 1912. A lively personal history, written more like a historical novel. Good for color and stories, poor history.

------------------. Rezanov. New York, 1906. A romantic account of one of the most famous romances in history, good for local color during the Spanish period.

Bailey, Paul. Sam Brannan and the California Mormons. Los Angeles, 1943.

Baldridge, William. The Days of 1846. San Francisco, 1877. A personal account of that period, dictated by the author.

Bancroft, Herbert Howe. History of California. San Francisco, 1884.

A multi-volume set, very detailed, by one of the foremost historians of the nineteenth century and certainly the definitive work on California to that period.

Battu, Zoe. "Tin Types," Sketches in the San Franciscan. San Francisco, 1927-1929.

Barry, T.A. Men and Memories of San Francisco. San Francisco, 1873.

Bean, Walton. Boss Ruef's San Francisco: The Story of the Union Labor Party, Big Business, and the Graft Prosecution. Berkeley, 1952. Indispensable for politics and corruption around the turn of the century. The definitive work.

Beechey, Frederick William. Narrative of a Voyage to the Pacific and Beering's Strait, to Cooperate with the Polar Expeditions: performed in His Majesty's Ship Blossom, Under the command of Captain F.W. Beechey. . .in the Years 1825, 26, 27, 28. London, 1831. Of value for the author's glimpses of the Mexican town of San Francisco.

Billington, Ray Allen. The Far Western Frontier. New York, 1956. Good background book for California and the West in general.

Bollens, John C. The Problem of Government in the San Francisco Bay Region. Berkeley, 1948.

Bolton, Herbert Eugene. Anza's California Expeditions, 1774, 1776. Berkeley, 1930. The best work on Anza by one of the West's finest historians.

--------------------. Crespi, Missionary Explorer. Berkeley, 1927.

--------------------. Fray Juan Crespi, Missionary Explorer on the Pacific Coast, 1769-1774. Berkeley, 1927.

--------------------. Historical Memoirs of New California. . .by Fray Francisco O.F.M. Translated from the manuscript in the archives by H.E. Bolton. Berkeley, 1926. Four volumes. If you want the original.

--------------------. An Outpost of Empire. New York, 1965. A glorified, romantic account, shows Spain as the bringer of civilization, not as good as his other books.

Brandon, William. The Men and the Mountain: Fremont's Fourth Expedition. New York, 1955.

Byington, Lewis Francis. The History of San Francisco. Chicago, 1931. Three volumes; one is narrative, the others are biographical sketches. Not very valuable.

Camp, William Martin. San Francisco Port of Gold. New York, 1947. An account of the waterfront written by a newspaper reporter. Many stories, not scholarly.

Canfield, Chauncey L. The Diary of a Forty Niner. Boston, 1920. What it says is interesting.

Chamisso, Albert von. A Sojourn at San Francisco Bay in 1816. San Francisco, 1936. An account of the Russian visit.

City of San Francisco. Manual of the Corporation of the City of San Francisco. San Francisco, 1852. Contains the first charter of the city.

Cross, William T., and Cross, Dorothy. A History of the Labor Movement in California. Berkeley, 1935. Good for as far as it goes.

Dana, Richard Henry. Two Years Before the Mast. New York, 1909. Known to all and often quoted, but very valuable for his description of the city in the early nineteenth century.

Delano, Alonzo. Pen Knife Sketches or Chips off the Old Block. San Francisco, 1934. Another personal account of the 1850's.

Department of the Interior. Report on the San Francisco Earthquake and Fire of 1906. Washington, 1906. The official report.

Dobie, Charles Caldwell. San Francisco: A Pageant. New York, 1939. Very good for the early period up to 1912 although he follows Elderedge quite closely. Perhaps its best value is a vivid description of the sections of the city and his inclusion of primary material.

Drake, Francis. World Encompassed. London, 1926. The story of the famous voyage, only useful to us for the discovery of Drake's Bay.

Du Four, Clarence John. The Russians in California. San Francisco, 1933. For serious students who wish to understand the interaction between the Spanish and Russians that led to the founding of the city.

Dwinelle, John W. Colonial History of City and County of San Francisco. San Francisco, 1866.

Edwards, Philip L. The Diary of Philip Leget Edwards. San Francisco, 1932.

Eldredge, Zoeth S. Beginnings of San Francisco from the Expedition of Anza, 1774 to the City Charter of April 15, 1850. San Francisco, 1912. A fine book for a short detailed history of the city to 1850. Far superior to his five-volume history of California.

Eldredge, Zoeth S. History of California. New York, 1914. Five volumes.

Eliel, Paul. The Waterfront and General Strikes. San Francisco, 1934. Basic for an understanding of that event.

Englehardt, O.F.M., Fr. Zephyrin. San Francisco or Mission Dolores. Chicago, 1924.

Flynn, William. Men, Money and Mud: The Story of San Francisco International Airport. San Francisco, 1954.

Font, Pedro. Font's Complete Diary. Translated and edited by Herbert Eugene Bolton, Berkeley, 1933.

Fremont, John Charles. Memoirs of My Life. Chicago, 1887. Not too much on San Francisco.

Gillis, William. Gold Rush Days with Mark Twain. New York, 1930. Well written interesting history of the gold rush days by a participant. Not too much on the city but good for the era.

Greenbie, Sydney, and Greenbie, Marjorie. Gold or Ophir. New York, 1925.

Hart, Jerome A. Our Second Century. San Francisco, 1931.

Hittell, John S. A History of the City of San Francisco and Incidentally of the State of California. San Francisco, 1878. Rather sketchy but has some material not found elsewhere.

Hughes, John T. California: An Account of the Revolution in California, 1846-7. Cincinnati, 1848. A first-hand account of that event, not too important for San Francisco.

James, Marquis, and James, Bessie R. Biography of a Bank: The Story of Bank of America. New York, 1954. Another specific book for the serious student.

Johnson, Kenneth M. San Francisco As it is: Being Gleanings from the Picayune, 1850-1852. Georgetown, California, 1964. A collection of stories that appeared in that paper, very fine.

Judnich, Martin W. San Francisco Government, A Summary of the San Francisco City and County Charter, the Laws and Ordinances, and the works of the Various Deparments. New York, 1967. The latest charter presented in outline form and explained to those who do not want to read the entire charter.

Keeler, Charles. San Francisco and Thereabout. San Francisco, 1902. Essays describing the life of the picturesque city by one of its boosters.

Kemble, Edward C. A History of California Newspapers 1846-1858, edited and annotated by Helen Harding Bretnor. Los Gatos, 1962. The definitive work on this subject.

Kinnard, Lawrence. History of the Greater San Francisco Bay Region. New York, 1966. A detailed two-volume work. Its major advantage or drawback is that it covers the entire bay region and is written with a rightist slant, but very well researched with an extremely valuable bibliography.

Kipling, Rudyard. Letters From San Francisco. San Francisco, 1949.

Kneiss, Gilbert H. Bonanza Railroads. Stanford, 1941.

Kotzebue, Otto von. A Voyage of Discovery, into the South Sea and Beering's Straits, for the Purpose of Exploring a Northeast Passage, Undertaken in the Years 1815-1818 at the Expense of His Highness. . .Count Romanzoff, in the Ship "Rurick," under the Command of the Lieutanant in the Russian Imperial Navy, Otto von Kotzebue. London, 1821. Three volumes. Of interest for his visit to San Francisco.

Langsdorff, George von Heinrich. Voyages and Travels. San Francisco, 1927.

The Laws of the Town of San Francisco, 1847. San Marino, 1947. The first pamphlet printed in English in California. Of great value to the student on many levels.

Lewis, Oscar. San Francisco: Mission to Metropolis. Berkeley, 1966. A small but highly readable narrative with many first-hand documents. Its main problem is that it is not very good for the modern period.

--------------. This Was San Francisco: Being First-Hand Accounts of the Evolution of One of America's Favorite Cities. New York, 1962.

Lloyd, B.F. Lights and Shades in San Francisco. San Francisco, 1876.

Markham, Edwin. California the Wonderful. New York, 1914.

Millard, Bailey. History of the San Francisco Bay Region. San Francisco, 1924. Three volumes, two are biography and one is narrative.

Moore, Ernest Carroll. California's Educators. Los Angeles, 1950.

Morrell, Benjamin. Narrative of Four Voyages to the South Sea, North and South Pacific Ocean, Chinese Sea, Ethiopic and Southern Atlantic Ocean, Indian and Antartic Ocean. . .From the Year 1822 to 1831. New York, 1832. Just read the parts about San Francisco.

Neuhaus, Eugen. The Art of the Exposition. San Francisco, 1915.

Nevins, Allan. Fremont, The West's Greatest Adventurer. New York, 1928. Two volumes. Probably the best work on Fremont.

O'Shaughnessey, Michael M. Hetch-Hetchy: Its Origin and History. San Francisco, 1934. For those interested in the development of the water system.

Paine, Swift. Eilley Orrum. Indianapolis, 1929.

Phillips, Catherine Coffin. Portsmouth Plaza, The Cradle of San Francisco. San Francisco, 1932.

Quiett, Glen Chesney. They Built the West: An Epic of Rails and Cities. New York, 1934.

Rae, W.F. Westward by Rail. London, 1871.

Riesenberg, Felix. Golden Gate: The Story of San Francisco Harbor. New York, 1940.

Robinson, Alfred. Life in California before the Conquest. San Francisco, 1925.

Rourke, Constance. Troopers of the Gold Coast. New York, 1928.

Royce, Josiah. California. Boston, 1886.

Russailh, Albert Bernard de. Last Adventure, San Francisco in 1831. San Francisco, 1931. Translated from the French by Clarkson Crane, contains witty and perceptive observations of an intelligent Frenchman, one of the best contemporary reports available.

San Francisco. Eradicating Plague from San Francisco. San Francisco, 1909. They wrote the book on how to eradicate plague. Valuable for that.

Scherer, James A.B. "The Lion of the Vigilantes," William T. Coleman and the Life of Old San Francisco. Indianapolis, 1939. Very good for the "law and order" group.

Sherman, William T. Memoirs of General William T. Sherman. New
    York, 1879. Sherman was stationed in San Francisco and his
    memoirs are valuable for a vivid picture of the city.

Soule, Frank; Gihon, John H. M.D.; and Nisbet, James. The Annals of
    San Francisco. New York, 1855. A classic work on the early
    period.

Sutter, John A. New Helvetia Diary. A Record kept by John A. Sutter
    and his clerks at New Helvetia, California, from September 9,
    1845 to May 28, 1848. San Francisco, 1939. Dull, but the gold
    rush started here.

Taper, Bernard Ed., Mark Twain's San Francisco. New York, 1963.
    A collection of the famous humorist's writings while he was in
    San Francisco and gold mining in the west.

Thomes, William H. On Land and Sea. Chicago, 1892.

Vancouver, George. Voyage of Discovery to the North Pacific Ocean,
    and round the World. . .Performed in the Years 1790, 1791,
    1792, 1793, 1794, and 1795, in the "Discovery" Sloop of War,
    and Armed Tender "Chatham," under the Command of Captain
    George Vancouver. London, 1798. Three volumes. Only of interest
    to the specialist.

Walpole, Frederick. Four Years in the Pacific, In Her Majesty's Ship
    "Collingwood" from 1844 to 1848. London, 1849. Two volumes.

Wierzbicki, F.P. California as It is and as It may be: or a Guide to the
    Gold Fields. San Francisco, 1850.

Wilkes, Charles. Narrative of the United States Exploring Expeditions,
    1838-1842. Philadelphia, 1845.

Williams, Mary Floyd. History of the San Francisco Committee of
    Vigilance of 1851. Berkeley, 1921. Outstanding example of original
    historical research, and sociological eveluation. The definitive
    history of the vigilance committee and one of the best histories
    of the city to 1854.

Young, John P. San Francisco: A History of the Pacific Coast Met-
    ropolis. San Francisco, 1914. A detailed two-volume history of the
    city, quite good as far as it goes.

NAME INDEX

Alemany, Archbishop Joseph Sadoc, 14
Alexander I (Czar), 3

Bancroft, George, 7
Bancroft, Herbert Howe, 19
Barnes, George E., 18
Barstow, Virginia, 29
Bartlett, Alan, 8
Bartlett, Washington A., 9
Bierce, Ambrose, 20
Big Brother and the Holding Company, 49
Bonaparte, Napoleon, 3
Boxton, Charles, 33
Brannan, Sam, 8, 10
Bridges, Harry, 46
Brown, Edmund, 48
Bryant, Andrew J., 24
Bryant, Edwin, 9
Buckley, Chris, 27

Cabrillo, Juan Rodrigus, 1
Cahill, B.J.S., 29
Casey, James P., 17, 18
Catherine II, 1
Cermeno, Sebastian Rodrigues, 1
Chiang kai-Shek, Madame, 44
Choyniski, Joe, 27
Coleman, William T., 18, 25
Corbett, James J., 27, 28, 31
Crespi, Father, 2
Crocker, Charles, 20
Crocker, Sewell, 31

Dana, Richard Henry, 6, 19
De Anza, Juan Bautista, 2
De Avala, Juan Manuel, 2
de Haro, Francisco, 5, 6
de Monterey, Conde, 1
de Portola, Gaspar, 1-2
Drake, Sir Francis, 1
Dunne, Frank H. 35

Echeandia, Jose Maria, 4
Eisenhower, Dwight, 47
Emperor Norton I, 22

Fages, Pedro, 2
Fillmore, Millard, 13
Fremont, John, 8
Francis, Saint, 3
Fremont, John, 8
Funston, General, 32

Gage, Henry T., 30
Gali, Francisco, 1
Galino, Jose, 5
Geary, John W., 12
George, Henry, 20
Giannini, Amadeo Peter, 31
Goldwater, Barry, 48
Grateful Dead, The, 49

Haight, Governor, 22
Hallidie, Andrew S., 16
Harte, Bret, 20
Haskell, Burnett, 27
Hoover, Herbert, 40
Hopkins, Mark, 20
Huntington, Collis, 20
Hyde, George, 9

Jackson, Andrew, 6
Jackson, H. Nelson, 31
Jeffries, Jim, 31
Johnson, J. Neely, 18
Johnston, Albert Sidney, 20
Jones, Commodore, 7
Joplin, Janis, 49
Judah, Theodore Dehone, 16

Kalloch, James, 26
Kearney, Dennis D., 25
Kimmel, Admiral, 44
King, James, 17, 18
Kotzebue, Otto von, 4

Larkin, Thomas O., 5
Lincoln, Abraham, 22
Logan, Mae Ella Hunt, 39

MacArthur, Douglas, 46
McCarthy, P.H., 34
McKenzie, Robert, 15

McKinley, Andrew, 29
McLaren, John, 44
Marshall, James, 10
Marston, J.D., 8
Mason, Richard, 10
Matson, William, 27
Meiggs, "Honest" Harry, 17
Morega, Jose Joaquin, 2
Morrell, Benjamin, 4
Moya y Contreras, Pedro, 1

Nixon, Richard M., 47
Nobili, John, 14

O'Farrell, Jasper, 9
Olson, Culbert L., 43
Ortega, Jose, 2

Palou, Father Francisco, 2
Partride, John, 31
Phelan, James Duval, 28, 30
Pio Pico, Don, 7
Pius, Saint, 3
Polk, James K., 7, 8

Reagan, Ronald, 50
Rezanov, Nicolai Petrovich, 3
Richardson, Captain A., 5
Ridley, Robert, 7
Ringgold, Lieutenant, 6
Robinson, Elmer, 46
Roosevelt, Franklin D., 42
Roosevelt, Theodore, 25
Ruef, Abe, 31, 34

Sanchez, Jose, 7
Sanders, Beverly, 13
Schmitz, Eugene A., 31, 33, 34
Scripps, E.W. 31
Serra, Father Junipero, 2
Shelley, J.F., 48
Slidell, John, 7
Sloat, Commodore John D., 7, 8
Smith, Jedediah, 4
Spofford, W.E., 12
Stanford, J.W., 27
Stanford, Leland, 20
Stevens, William, 37
Stockton, Robert F., 8
Strauss, Levi, 13
Stuart, James, 15
Sullivan, Father John W., 36
Sullivan, John L., 28
Sumner, General E.V., 20
Sutro, Adolph, 28
Sutter, John Augustus, 6, 10

Taft, William Howard, 32, 34
Taylor, Edward T., 33
Truman, Harry S, 46
Twain, Mark, 20, 22
Tyler, John, 6

Vancouver, George, 3
Vioget, 6

Walker, William, 16
Weinberg, Jack, 48
Whittaker, Samuel, 15
Wilson, Woodrow, 36, 37